10.99

BLUEPRINTS

Religious Education
Key Stage 1
Teacher's Resource
Book

D0352258

CR
200
BLU

Stanley Thornes (Publishers) Ltd

Do you receive BLUEPRINTS NEWS?

Blueprints is an expanding series of practical teacher's ideas books and photocopiable resources for use in primary schools. Books are available for separate infant and junior age ranges for every core and foundation subject, as well as for an ever widening range of other primary teaching needs. These include **Blueprints Primary English** books and **Blueprints Resource Banks**. **Blueprints** are carefully structured around the demands of National Curriculum in England and Wales, but are used successfully by schools and teachers in Scotland, Northern Ireland and elsewhere.

Blueprints provide :
- *Total curriculum coverage*
- *Hundreds of practical ideas*
- *Books specifically for the age range you teach*
- *Flexible resources for the whole school or for individual teachers*
- *Excellent photocopiable sheets - ideal for assessment and children's work profiles*
- *Supreme value*

Books may be bought by credit card over the telephone and information obtained on **(0242) 228888**. Alternatively, photocopy and return this **FREEPOST** form to receive **Blueprints News**, our regular update on all new and existing titles. You may also like to add the name of a friend who would be interested in being on the mailing list.

Please add my name to the **BLUEPRINTS NEWS** mailing list.

Mr/Mrs/Miss/Ms --

Home address --

--Postcode ------------------------

School address --

-- Postcode ------------------------

Please also send **BLUEPRINTS NEWS** to :

Mr/Mrs/Miss/Ms --

Address --

-- Postcode ------------------------

To: Marketing Services Dept., Stanley Thornes Ltd, FREEPOST (GR 782), Cheltenham, GL50 1BR

First published in 1993 by:
Stanley Thornes (Publishers) Ltd
Ellenborough House
Wellington Street
CHELTENHAM GL50 1YD

Reprinted 1994

A catalogue record for this book is available from the British Library

0–7487–1636–X

Typeset by Tech-Set, Gateshead, Tyne & Wear
Printed and bound in Great Britain at The Bath Press, Avon

CONTENTS

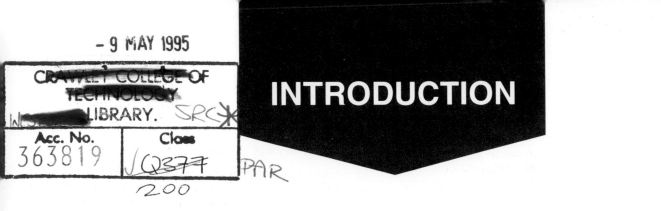

INTRODUCTION

What is Blueprints *Religious Education*?

Blueprints *Religious Education* is a practical classroom resource for primary RE that may be used as either a structured core course or a flexible resource.

At each Key Stage it consists of a Teacher's Resource Book, a photocopiable pupils' book and a cassette. Together these provide a complete resource, although it is not necessary to have all the components to use the material profitably. **Blueprints** *Religious Education* is carefully structured. It provides coherent learning objectives designed to enable you to fulfil your statutory RE objectives and to deliver a broad and balanced syllabus for RE.

For each Key Stage there are nine topics as follows.

Key Stage 1

- Big Me and Little Me
- Birth celebrations
- Food
- Worship
- Beliefs and lifestyles
- Sacred books
- Beginnings
- The natural world
- Friendship

Key Stage 2

- My wonderful mind
- Let's celebrate
- Let's communicate
- The God we worship
- We believe
- Sacred lives
- Endings
- Let's protect
- Other people count

Key Stages 1 and 2 together offer a continuous and progressive programme of learning.

The nine topics at each Key Stage have been tailored to provide a complete 'off-the-peg' RE curriculum, with a topic per term at Key Stage 1. Although the topics can be used in any order there is a general progression in levels of difficulty and in learning objectives throughout the books. Big Me and Little Me is, of course, an ideal reception starting point, whereas later topics are more suitable for older infants.

Blueprints and the RE curriculum

Blueprints *Religious Education* will help you to achieve the statutory requirements to teach RE as set out in the Educational Reform Act 1988. The legal position of RE is as follows:

- RE is part of the 'Basic' but not the 'National' Curriculum
- RE must be taught in all state-maintained schools
- the content of RE must reflect Britain's Christian tradition while taking into consideration the major religious traditions represented in Great Britain
- RE must be taught according to a locally prescribed Agreed Syllabus which is presented by a Standing Conference formed by Standing Advisory Councils for Religious Education, a mandatory group established in response to the 1988 Reform Act.

The 1988 Reform Act made mandatory the setting up of Standing Advisory Councils for Religious Education (SACRE) whose main purpose is to advise the Education Authorities concerning all matters in connection with RE and collective worship, with particular regard to the Agreed Syllabus for RE. The latter must be reviewed by SACRE and where appropriate a Standing Conference be convened to produce a new Agreed Syllabus which will meet the needs of the Reform Act's requirements in the local area.

Blueprints *Religious Education* seeks to provide material which would be considered appropriate to all aspects of the Reform Act's requirements. The approach to RE in **Blueprints** is initially implicit rather than directly related to particular faiths: that is to say, the starting point for work is children's own personal awareness of family, self and childhood experiences. Birthdays, food, nature and friendship are all important themes at Key Stage 1. Gradually information and activities about different faiths are added. The approach to faiths is broad and all the major religions are introduced in simple terms at Key Stage 1. Christianity, however, is given a leading role in the books in line with the legal requirements. You will find an index starting on page 106 of all the activities, stories and copymasters that relate to each of the faiths in case you wish to find material for any one particular faith.

Whereas the accepted guidance on appropriate time to be allotted to RE in any school curriculum has been 5 per cent, it is usual at Key Stage 1 for children to be involved in topic work concerning several areas of study and for RE to be included in this integrated approach. One of the purposes of this book is to provide topics in which RE can be easily linked with National Curriculum subjects.

The Teacher's Resource Book

The Teacher's Resource Book is the core of **Blueprints** *Religious Education* and can be used on its own without the copymasters or the cassette. It offers the following resources for each of the nine topics:

- a clear set of learning objectives which outline the RE objectives of the topic
- a flow chart mapping out the learning of the topic
- a set of starting points to get practical work going
- a number of areas of study with clearly defined purposes and a large bank of practical, structured activities
- a collection of stories to read alongside the activities.

The activities draw widely on cross-curricular skills, and all the subjects of the National Curriculum may be explored through the nine topics. There is plentiful scope for storytelling, writing, mapwork, graphing and data collection, music, drama and artwork, but these skills are always used in a purposeful way to further defined RE objectives. **Blueprints** *Religious Education* is a focused RE resource, not a cross-curricular package with some RE thrown in.

There is scope throughout for assessment and self-assessment of RE learning. This is usually through the copymasters, and you will find these opportunities for self-assessment identified in the book through the use of this logo:

Opportunities for assessment and self-assessment provide an integral part of the chosen material.

Topic songs

You will also find that there is a song accompanying each topic which directly relates to the chosen theme and introduces the children to the topic, providing an enjoyable cross-curricular focus to their term's work. The written music and lyrics can be found in the copymasters.

The cassette

The cassette provides recorded versions of the songs consisting of:

- a complete version of voice and accompaniment, which you can listen to with the children to learn the words and melody
- accompaniment only for the children to sing to.

The cassette can also be used effectively as part of an assembly coming out of the topic work. You will find reference to the use of the cassette in the Teacher's Resource Book by this symbol:

The copymasters

You will find reference to the copymasters in the Teacher's Resource Book by this symbol:

The copymasters provide a bank of pupil activities for use alongside the Teacher's Resource Book. The activities are wide ranging in their skills, drawing on English, Maths, Geography and Art. Many of them provide pages that can be cut up into booklets and they also have a self-assessment function as mentioned earlier. At the front of the pupils' book you will find the music for each of the topic songs together with the words for possible pupil use with older Key Stage 1 children.

Big Me and Little Me

Myself, my thoughts, my feelings

- Myself – am I of value to anyone?
- How to cope with negative feelings in a positive way
- Changing the way we think
- Think before you speak
- Being thoughtful in what we say and do

Taking care of others

- Taking care of others
- Sharing
- Animals count too
- Other people who care

Helping others

- Being helpful
- Using all of ourselves to help others

BIG ME AND LITTLE ME

Trusting

- Trusting

Caring for the community

- People all around us
- What people do for us
- What we can do for them

Listening

- Listening carefully
- Listening to 'conscience'

1

LEARNING OBJECTIVES

- To be aware of our changing moods and feelings, and to consider the reasons for feeling sad, angry, happy, etc.
- To be aware of the effects that our moods have on others, and their moods upon us.
- To accept the fact that other people may look at situations quite differently from us, and hold opposite opinions.
- To be aware of the effect that the environment, especially weather conditions, can have on our feelings and moods.
- To learn strategies to help overcome negative communication with others.

STARTING POINTS

- Show the class some pictures of people in different situations, obtained from magazines, posters or photographs. What do the children think these people are feeling like? For example, a bride and bridegroom (happy), a tramp (lonely), a child opening a Christmas present (excited), two people fighting (angry), someone crying (sad), etc. Discuss how the children themselves are feeling at present, and ask them to explain why.

- Sit with the children in an informal area of the classroom. Ask them to close their eyes and feel their faces methodically, starting with the forehead, eyebrows and eyes and working down to the nose, mouth and chin. When they open their eyes, invite them to 'pull faces' to show different emotions. Tell them you want them to feel happy and ask them what has happened to their faces. Do the same for 'sad', 'angry', 'lonely', 'excited' and encourage children to feel the differences in expression in their own faces. Emphasise that the way we feel inside is reflected in our outer expression.

- Now give each child a large sheet of paper on which you have drawn two 'egg' shapes to represent two faces. Ask them to write their own name underneath the left-hand egg shape and a friend's name underneath the right-hand egg shape. They should then draw their own facial expression in the left-hand egg shape and the expression of their friend in the right-hand egg shape. Invite them to discuss with their friend both expressions: what do the faces tell us?

- Read the children a story about a family and consider with them friendships within the family. How do members show they care for each other? Do any of them share things? Who helps at home and how? Ask pupils to write accounts of their own families and illustrate them with photographs brought in from home. Encourage the children to talk about their families but be sensitive to those for whom family life may be a negative experience.

- Take the class on a walk around the local community. Show the children the church, the mosque, the hospital, the park and other landmarks. Ask them to think about what goes on at each place – who works there and what are they doing? Who is looking after these places for everyone? Talk about the different types of buildings you come across and point out that some were built a long time ago, others very recently. Explain that all buildings are designed according to the activities which take place within them: for example, home dwellings, schools, hospitals, leisure centres, etc. Ask them to describe the shapes and architectural features of buildings with special functions – hospitals, churches, mosques, schools, leisure centres, etc. Discuss the important role architects, designers and builders play in our community. On returning to school, if possible, watch a video about the local community to reinforce this area of learning.

- Teach the children the topic song, **Big Me**, to introduce the ideas to be studied in the forthcoming topic. Study the words together and think about their meaning.

MYSELF, MY THOUGHTS, MY FEELINGS

Purpose
To look at ourselves, examine our thoughts and feelings in various situations and how these might affect others.

Activity 1: Myself – am I of value to anyone?
A Sit with children informally and reintroduce the idea of Big Me and Little Me by showing two simple line drawings, one of a happy, smiling face (Big Me), the other of a cross, grumpy face (Little Me). Ask the children to describe the expressions: why does the happy face belong to Big Me and the sad face to Little Me? Could it be that Little Me has had an argument with Big Me? Have the children ever had an argument with somebody? What do they imagine they looked like?

Ask the children what else makes them cross and grumpy like Little Me, or smiling and happy like Big Me,

Family resemblances

and write down suggestions on the blackboard. Do pupils help others when they are cross and grumpy like Little Me? Are they of value if they smile at others as Big Me does? How can Big Me help to make other people happy?

B Ask the children to write a story where Big Me helps a person who is feeling like Little Me: suggest that this could be an unhappy brother or sister or somebody who is being unfriendly towards them. Pupils could draw or paint a picture of Big Me's and Little Me's faces. What do the expressions tell the children about the way Big Me and Little Me are feeling? They can then draw or paint pictures of themselves, their family, their friends. What do the expressions on these faces tell them? Consolidate this work by writing a class list of characteristics children have decided belong to Big Me and Little Me.

C Read the story **A shock for Teddy** (p. 11) to the children and talk about the relationships between the various toys. Why were Sindy and Barbie arguing? Why were the other toys affected by this? Examine different reactions given in the story. Focus on Teddy's personality with the children: why do they think the other toys looked up to him? Why could he not 'believe his ears' at the end of the story?

Divide the class into several groups and act out or mime short scenes which have Big Me or Little Me in them. These could be based on real-life experiences or made up from stories and other sources. After a limited time the whole class could watch each group's scene and discuss what happened.

D Look at photographs of pupils with their families and identify family resemblances between children and their mother, father, brother, sister, aunt, uncle, etc. Explain that we inherit certain characteristics from our families but, while we have many similarities on the outside, we all have different talents inside which we can use to help others. We must use our eyes and look carefully at ourselves and those around us in order to learn about each other on the inside and not just rely on our physical appearance.

✔ Give out **Copymaster 1** (How is Freddie Face feeling?). The children should fill in the blanks with words given in the opening sentence. They can

then draw their own facial expression and features and write down a word to describe how they are feeling in the box provided. Make sure the word matches the expression.

Activity 2: Feelings – negative to positive
A Play the children music which evokes positive feelings (calm, joy, peace) and negative feelings (anger, sadness, fear). Discuss how the music made them feel. What music makes them feel happy or sad? Can they give you examples? Do they think playing music influences people's feelings?

Tell the children to experiment with percussion instruments and their voices and in groups make up sounds to express different feelings. Give an example of how this can be done. Give each group a title ('happy', 'angry', etc.) but ask them to keep the name of their sound-piece a secret. After some rehearsal they can perform their piece to the rest of the class who can guess what mood or feelings are being conveyed through the music. Did the way in which the children played their instruments give the others a clue? What was the expression on their faces like? Did this help the others to guess the mood of the piece? Which groups were playing Little Me's moods and which were playing Big Me's moods?

B Read **The Prophet Muhammad and the lady with the rubbish** (p. 12) to the children. Afterwards, ask the class how Muhammad treated the lady who was angry with him. Did they find Muhammad's actions surprising? Why? How could the children tell from the story that Muhammad was a kind man?

Invite pupils to draw a picture in their workbooks and write a few sentences about an occasion when they have felt angry. What words would they choose to describe their feelings in the picture? What did they do to stop themselves feeling angry? Write short stories about other negative or uncomfortable feelings. What did pupils do to make themselves and those around them feel better? Can they write about a time when they assisted a person around them who needed help but was unfriendly like the lady in the story? How did they overcome the feeling of not being wanted? Did they become friends afterwards? Why?

In groups, role-play situations where somebody like the lady with the rubbish needs help. How do they

approach the angry person to offer help? Is the help accepted and how do both parties react?

C Show photographs of people looking angry, happy, upset, laughing, etc., then ask the children to paint pictures of the following characters: Susan Sad, Jimmy Lonely, Mr Laughter, Mrs Grumpy. Pupils should think carefully before drawing the expressions.

D When the children have watched an argument taking place, have they ever looked at the faces of the people arguing? What did the people's voices sound like? Pupils can experiment with their voices and produce the different sounds that we recognise as expressing certain feelings: for example, shouting when angry, quiet sobbing when crying, soft, gentle sounds when whispering, etc. Pupils can write these descriptive words down. What other sounds can they hear?

Activity 3: Changing the way we think
A Read the story **Changing the way we think** (p. 13). Consider with the children if they have ever rushed into doing or saying something without thinking and then regretted it afterwards. Return to the story and ask them why it was that the teacher, in writing good things about her pupils, changed the way they thought and behaved afterwards. Ask the children what they would do to help a friend who was feeling upset.

B Sit the children informally in a group close to a display of toys which you have asked them to bring into school. Encourage them to point out to each other the names of the toys and how they work. Would they be willing to share their toys with anyone in the class? What would happen if someone did not want to share a toy? How would the others feel? Help the children to write a story about a time when they visited a friend's house and when a friend visited their house. Were they able to share their friend's toys and share their own toys with their friend?

C Divide the class into small groups and ask them to mime short scenes with their friends where they react

to a situation in a negative way because they had not stopped to think first – just like Bobby in the story who would not share his sweets or Jenny who was always rude. They should then mime the scene again, this time making the ending different because the children had stopped to think and considered what to do for the best.

D Ask the class to draw or paint four faces representing the following expressions: angry, sad, thoughtful, happy. Each face should be the same and only the expression should change. The children can write down the words under the expressions on the faces in the right order.

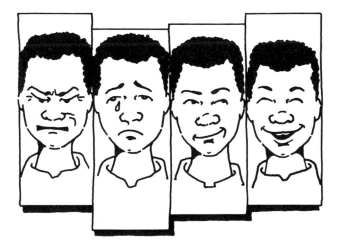

They can then paint large 'mood pictures', carefully deciding what colours might be chosen for the following themes: 'happiness', 'sadness', 'thoughtfulness', 'anger' and 'peace'. Explore the effect of colour upon mood before attempting this exercise. Here are some colour–mood associations:

- red – angry
- pink – happy
- brown – unhappy
- blue – calm
- yellow – cheerful
- green – soothing.

E Use **Copymaster 2** (Do I stop to think?), showing six pictures of children in different situations, namely fighting, sharing, showing friendship, arguing, pushing and making friends again after a disagreement. Talk about the pictures and invite pupils to tick the ones which show the children who have stopped to think about how their actions affect others and put a cross by those showing selfish, inconsiderate behaviour. Pupils can then colour the pictures in which the characters have stopped to think, cut them out and stick them in their workbooks, accompanied by appropriate captions. Use this as an opportunity to reflect upon how the children speak to their friends. Do they upset people? Do they think before they speak to their family and friends and does the way they speak influence others' responses?

Emphasise the importance of sharing in friendship. Ask the children to draw or list those things which they share with their friends. Can they add any items which they would like to share in the future?

F Read the story **The echo** (p. 13). Why does Joanna have no friends but prefers to spend her time with grown-ups instead? Why did her feelings change at the end of the story? Why did she become friendly?

Ask the children to write about an incident, real or imaginary, where something happens to change a friend's outlook and behaviour for the better. Encourage them to work in groups to role-play their stories and discuss how being friendly can transform people's lives.

HELPING OTHERS C3–4

Area of study 2.

Purpose
To become aware of how we can be of help to others in various situations and avoid negative communication in our lives.

Activity 1: Being helpful
A Ask pupils to draw or paint a picture of a child in the class helping someone, choosing the situation

carefully. Can pupils explain why they chose their scene and why they think it was important to help out?

Have children ever been asked to do something, said yes, but then not bothered to do it? Is this being helpful? Are they always careful to do something when asked? How do other people react when they let them down? Think of different ways of helping others at home or at school. Pupils can write a short story about when they helped someone, explaining how the person reacted and how it made them feel.

B Sit the children in a circle and ask them to hold hands. Explain to them that this is touching and through touching we can communicate with other people and animals and show we care for them, bringing us closer together. Talk about the different ways in which hands are used for communication: for example, holding, stroking, writing, healing, touching, feeling, saying sorry and praying.

Do we handle things around us with enough care? Ask the children to practise handling objects in the classroom. Do they think enough about the way they should be handled? When we open a book do we do it carefully and feel it is something to be used with respect? Find examples of how holy books are handled and discuss these with the children: for example, the Qu'ran is held in a piece of paper so the book itself is not touched. Why are holy books treated in such a way?

Hands are for......

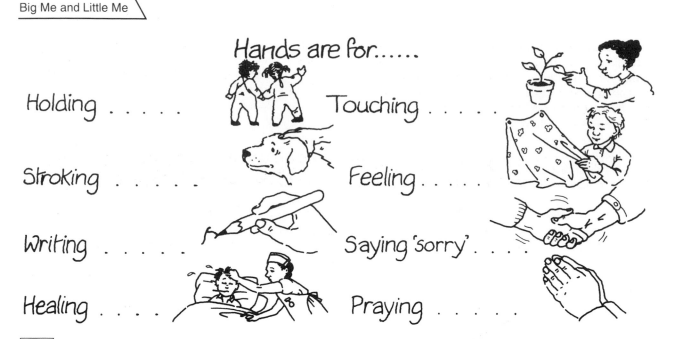

Holding . . . . .

Stroking . . . . .

Writing . . . . . .

Healing . . . .

Touching . . . . .

Feeling . . . . .

Saying 'sorry' . . . .

Praying . . . . .

✓ Give out **Copymaster 3** (Using all of ourselves to help). First discuss with the children how many parts of their bodies they have used to help someone today. Then pupils can tick the boxes to record this and label the parts of the body on the figure drawing.

Activity 2: Sharing is being helpful

A Give out some books, one between two in the classroom. Point out to the children that they are now sharing a book. Do they like sharing a book with a friend? Does it make learning about what is in the book more fun? Are they helping their friend by sharing the book and talking about what is in it together? Remind them of their previous work on sharing (see p. 4) and ask the class what other things they might share with each other. Would they want to share these things with those who may not be their immediate friends? What would be the result of offering something to someone in the class who was not a close friend? Would this be a good idea? If so, why? Have the children made new friends through sharing?

B Read the story of the feeding of the five thousand (John 6:1–14). Tell the children afterwards to draw a picture in their workbooks and underneath write the story in their own words.

Act out or mime the scene showing the feeding of the five thousand. Can the children imagine the smell of the fish and fresh bread at the scene? Do they think that the food would have smelt and tasted good? Do the children think the food would have smelt and tasted even better to the youngster who gave his loaf and fish to Jesus? Why? Are we thankful for the taste of good food in daily life? Do we appreciate the smell of a meal being prepared? The children should then write down foods they particularly like and describe the sort of smells they sense from the kitchen. Does the smell make them feel more hungry?

C Ask pupils to bring in foods (or provide them with food) from different cultures. The children should taste the food and describe its taste as accurately as they can. What does the food smell like? What kind of food do children eat at festival times: for example, Christmas, Easter, Passover, Diwali, Chinese New Year? Where and how is it eaten? Why do the children who are given food at these times treat it with respect? Pupils can make a 'food share' booklet, showing the different foods that they eat and can offer to and share with their friends.

✓ Split the class into groups and give out **Copymaster 4** (The tasting and smelling game). Organise the game so that each child tastes and smells

'Food share' booklet

the samples under blindfold conditions. The children mark the 'Yes/No' column on the copymaster with a tick or cross where indicated to show whether they have recognised the sample or not. In the next column, they write down a word to describe the taste or smell of the sample. Afterwards, discuss with the children the results of the tests carried out in the groups, and make a class bar chart clearly showing the likes and dislikes of the food sampled.

Area of study 3.

LISTENING

C5

Purpose
To emphasise that it is important to listen carefully to what is being said and act accordingly.

Activity 1: Listening carefully
 A Play a tape to the children, previously discreetly recorded, of them chattering in class. What can the children hear? Can they hear and understand the talking? Point out that nobody can hear properly what is being said and if we are not listening carefully enough to each other when talking, we will miss something important, as everybody has something important to say.

B Talk about whether the class listen carefully enough to you, the teacher, and do what you ask them to do. Point out that in the past they have panicked because they have not known what to do, and this was possibly because they had not been listening to instructions. Ask them to give examples of when they have not been listening in other situations. For example, have they always listened to Mum when she has asked them to do something? Have they ever listened to the little voice inside them, the one we call 'conscience'? Write this word on the blackboard. What is 'conscience' telling us if we listen very carefully?

Activity 2: Listening and doing
A Ask the children to write down what they should do in the following situations in order for them to follow instructions correctly:

- the teacher asks them to collect all the workbooks at the end of the lesson
- their mother or father asks them to clear the table at the end of their evening meal
- the lollipop lady or man asks them to cross the road at a specific time
- a friend asks them to listen to a problem they might have.

B Read the children the story of Samuel and Eli (1 Samuel 3). Explain that the little boy listened carefully to God's instructions and because of this he received a very important message. Stress that if Samuel had not listened to the voice of God he would not have known that one day he himself would have been giving messages to all people in the land.

Show the class pictures of Samuel as a boy and later as a leader. Ask them to write the story as if they were Samuel perceiving and listening to the voice of God, and to write down the important message from God. Ask the children to draw pictures of Samuel as a boy from his bed hearing the voice of God. This can be followed by the children acting or miming the story of Samuel, hearing the voice of God in the temple. Did Eli believe Samuel was hearing the voice of God at first?

✔ Use **Copymaster 5** (Do I listen carefully?). Look at the four pictures and discuss their content. The children can then confirm what they have learnt from the pictures by describing them underneath in the space provided and are asked if they can think of anyone else they must listen to carefully.

Area of study 4

TRUSTING OTHERS

C6

Purpose
To show that trusting others produces positive feelings and results in good relationships.

Activity 1: Trusting others
 A Give a 20 pence coin to any child in your class and tell them you want them to look after it for you and give it back to you at the end of the day. Later, sit the children informally and tell them that you put your trust in somebody in the class to look after some money for you. Ask for the money back. When the child has produced it you praise them and tell them you are glad you could put your trust in them to look after the

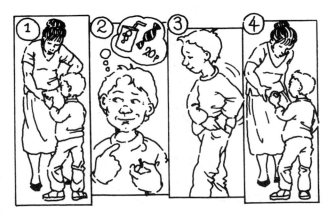

7

money. Ask the children what is meant by trust. How might they feel if someone put their trust in them?

B Read the story of Jesus with the little child (Matthew 18:1–6) and discuss it with the children. How do they know that the little child trusted Jesus? How did the child's trust in Jesus help the disciples who were with him? Pupils can draw a large picture of Jesus with the little child sitting on his knee.

C Ask the children if they have ever really stopped to think about whether the others in the class trust them as individuals. When might they need to trust each other?

How many people can they think of who put their trust in God to help them in their everyday lives? Write a list together on a large sheet of paper. Show them pictures or photographs of some of these people and, if possible, videos of adults and children at prayer.

D Pupils can write a story featuring Big Me and Little Me: Little Me finds himself in a situation where he has to ask Big Me to keep a secret. Did Little Me trust Big Me? Why? Did this make Little Me think that he should start to trust others? In groups, children can act out or mime their stories of trust and discuss the situations with the rest of the class.

E Attempt **Copymaster 6** (I trust . . .) where the children should draw four pictures of people whom they trust. Underneath the pictures they should name the characters and write a few sentences about each in the spaces provided. Ask the children to draw a large picture of themselves to display alongside their completed copymasters. Suggest to them that, while it is important to trust those whom they know, they should always be aware of their own feelings and trust in the judgements they make about others. Explain, with sensitivity, that it may be necessary to say 'no' not only to strangers but also to those close to them on some occasions.

Area of study 5

TAKING CARE OF OTHERS

C7

Purpose

To point out that it is for the good of others that we should take care of them and not just think about ourselves.

Activity 1: Taking care of others

A Obtain uniforms or items of clothing associated with people who play a major role in the welfare of children – a doctor, a nurse, a police officer, a lollipop lady or man, etc. Dress a number of children in the clothes and stand them in a row with a child in school uniform, if appropriate, at the end. Talk about what these people do to help us each day and point out that the child at the end can also do things to help. Do all these people show thoughtfulness and consideration for others?

B Can pupils give examples of how they have been helpful and cared for someone? Ask them to draw a picture of helping someone in need, either from real-life experience or from an imaginary situation. Sit with the children afterwards and talk about the pictures with the whole class discussing the content and highlighting any details pupils wish to emphasise. The pictures can then be displayed as a classroom frieze with appropriate labels.

C Read John 10:11–16, a biblical passage which talks about Jesus being the Good Shepherd who cares for his sheep. Ask the class how he cares for them? What does he say and do? Give examples from different faiths of caring attitudes towards others: for example, Muhammad and the animal stories, the Buddha and the Jataka stories, Guru Nanak and his caring for the poor and needy, etc.

Uniforms to help others

D The children could devise their own scenes in small groups where they are seen to be showing care for their friends or a stranger around them. Why did they think they should take care of the person? How did they help?

Activity 2: Animals count too

A Show the children pictures of many different types of animals. How many pupils have pets at home? If they do not own a pet, what pet would they like and why?

B Read stories about animals who have been looked after by their owners and how they have responded to this care in different situations. Read the children the story of 'Muhammad and the crying camel' (a well-known Islamic story to be found in *Guru Nanak and the Snake* by Ruth Parmiter and Monica Price – see Bibliography), where Muhammad notices a camel who has been ill-treated. What did Muhammad say to the owner to make him change his ways?

C Write a story about an animal who had strayed from home who was found, looking lost and wandering around in the road, by two children walking home from school. Describe the feelings of the animal when found and how it responded to being looked after.

Mime or act out scenes where children find an animal has been found ill or mistreated. Pupils can also mime or act out short scenes of grooming, cleaning, feeding and training animals. Afterwards, make a list of all the things that have to be done in order to look after a pet properly. Ask them what other ways, apart from practical ones, they can show animals that they care about them.

good food

love and care

exercise

gentle talking

a clean, comfortable home

careful handling

D Invite a representative from one of the animal welfare organisations to come into school and talk about the welfare of animals. If there is an animal sanctuary in your locality use this as an opportunity to arrange a visit.

✓ Provide pupils with **Copymaster 7** (Pet care). The children join the dots to make a picture of a dog and colour it in. Look at the small sketches of pet care with them and talk about each one. Number the boxes in order of importance when looking after a pet. The children can then colour in the pictures, cut them out and make a small booklet called 'Pet care', the last page of which could be a drawing of a pet they own or know.

| Area of study 6 | CARING FOR THE COMMUNITY | C8–10 |

Purpose
To show that through caring for the community in which we live and the people within it, we can live happily together.

Activity 1: People all around us

A Ask the children to think of all the people they can who help in their community and write a list on the blackboard. What do these people do – for example, doctor, nurse, dentist, teacher, firefighter, vicar, minister, priest, imam, rabbi?

Make a large collage on the wall of the people the children have thought of who help in their community.

B Show the children pictures of children praying. Where are they – in a church, a mosque, a synagogue, a temple, a community hall? Show the children large pictures of these places which they can then draw or paint on to the collage.

cotton wool clouds

HOSPITAL

flat cut-outs of buildings

POLICE STATION

LIBRARY

SCHOOL

flat cut-outs of figures

C Write simple poems about people who care in their community, using suitable words. Remind pupils of the pictures they have been looking at and describe what they look like. Who works there? What happens when we visit for regular acts of worship or on special occasions such as christenings, Bar Mitzvah – reading from holy books, praying, singing, or chanting praises? Write short descriptions of these activities and ones in which the children might actively take part: for example, singing songs, going to Sunday School or Junior Church, walking in processions, celebrating festivals such as Easter and Passover.

D What do the children who attend the different buildings do there? Ask the children to mime entering the buildings and taking part in appropriate activities: for example, a Muslim child entering, removing shoes and bowing; a Hindu child entering, removing shoes, taking food and singing; a Christian entering, kneeling and taking communion, etc.

E Remind the class that they have been learning about how using their five senses helps them to live a full and happy life, appreciating people and things around them. They can write a poem saying 'thank you' for this, including in it examples of how their five senses can be used in a caring way.

✓ **Copymaster 8** (My community) shows five people in the community and five buildings in which they work. The children can match the people with the buildings.

Activity 2: Our community

A Remind pupils of their visit to the local community (see **Starting points**) and list with them all the things they remember seeing on their visit.

Show the children a large, simplified aerial map of their community. Work out with them where you went on your visit. Can they find certain landmarks such as the main street, the park, the town square, etc.? Can they find the street where they live? Duplicate the aerial map and give the children reduced copies for their books or folders. Ask them to label with a small cross where they live, the nearest church or place of worship to their house, the nearest hospital, library, etc. They can colour in the trees green, the roads red and the buildings yellow, etc. – you can devise with them a suitable colour scheme for the whole community. Pupils can also work out the direction they have to walk in from school to home, home to the town centre, home to a friend's house, etc. Finally, you may wish to ask questions about the layout of the community: for example, why is the hospital in a busy part of town? Does this help people who visit there?

Copymaster 9 (All around me) shows a map which might be similar to your community. Mark on the copymaster the route from the school to the library (in red), the school to the leisure centre (in blue), the school to the mosque (in green), the church to the cinema (in brown), and any other appropriate routes. Ask the children the shape of the library, the park, the cinema, the leisure centre, and so on.

B Make a classroom miniature model community. With your help, the children can make an aerial map in the form of a floormat, while cut-out figures representing all the people they can think of who help in their community can be made out of cardboard and buildings can be constructed out of balsa wood, shoe-boxes and cartons. The figures can be positioned near to the building they belong to.

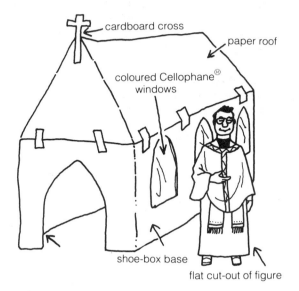

cardboard cross
paper roof
coloured Cellophane® windows
shoe-box base
flat cut-out of figure

C Make a wall frieze near the miniature model community and on it place flat cut-outs of the same people that appear in the model miniature community. Now add cut-outs of all the children in the class. Explain that this shows that we all belong together and need each other to make the community we live in a good place; everybody counts and we should all care about each other and the place in which we live.

D Make large posters using a variety of materials and carrying a 'caring message': for example: 'Smile – it feels good!' 'Be happy – the sun's shining!' 'Don't drop litter!' Display the posters in a school corridor for other pupils to see.

E Make some sounds using objects in the classroom. Ask the children to describe these sounds – loud, soft, ringing, banging, etc. Now ask the class what sounds we

drip! rustle tap! clang! scrape! rattle! ring! jangle!

hear every day in our community. List with the children sounds made at home (talking, banging, whistling, barking, mewing, telephone ringing, door bell sounding, radio/stereo/television playing, pots rattling, machines churning) and sounds made at school (school bell ringing, chattering, somebody turning over the page of a book, eating lunch, singing in assembly). Finally, a list could be compiled of sounds made in the street (traffic noise – different pitches such as a bus growling, a car whizzing past or blasting its horn – weather noise, rattling milkbottles, refuse collecting, people walking or running for a bus.

✓ On **Copymaster 10** (What sound is around?), eight sounds from the environment have to be identified and one has been done as an example. Children should draw a picture of the object from where the sound comes and an imaginative 'picture' of the

sound, then write the name of the object in the appropriate column. They can invent their own sound from the environment and record this on the copymaster in the same way.

TOPIC STORIES ▶

A shock for Teddy

Barbie, the dark-haired doll and pretty, blonde Sindy were having an argument. The other toys were not really listening at first. The two dolls didn't like each other very much and often quarrelled.

'What's the trouble this time?' asked Sammy, the clockwork dog, from his shelf in the toy cupboard. 'Has Katie bought Sindy another dress and Barbie wants one too?'

'It's not that,' answered Kite, who had been left on the floor on the landing and could hear the dolls through Katie's bedroom door. 'They're arguing about which of them will be put in the dustbin.'

'Oh!' Thomas the Tank Engine, who had been left on his track all evening by little Carl, laughed at Kite. 'Katie's mum will have said that if she doesn't look after her toys properly, they'll be thrown in the bin. I've heard her say that before.'

'It's more than that,' replied Kite. 'The children's Mum is always saying that, but she doesn't mean it. This is much worse by the sound of it.'

'Ask Teddy if he knows,' said Sammy. 'He knows everything.'

Teddy didn't know. 'No one's said anything in front of me,' he told them. 'Why don't we ask Computer? He might know.'

'Computer doesn't think he's one of us,' Kite reminded him. 'Remember how lonely he was when he first came and how we helped him. He just ignores us now.'

'Well then, you'll have to ask Barbie and Sindy to tell us,' advised Teddy, 'when you can get a word in, that is.'

Kite waited until Barbie and Sindy paused for breath.

'Will you two girls come into the baby's room and tell us what's going on?' asked Kite politely.

Barbie and Sindy walked importantly into the small bedroom where the baby lay fast asleep. The toy cupboard was next to the cot and they opened the door quietly.

'What do you want?' asked Barbie in a cross voice.

'Kite said something about you being thrown in the dustbin,' said Teddy at once.

'Not me, I'm too important.'

Barbie took a comb from the little bag she carried and combed her long hair.

'Not me, either. Katie's only just got me for her birthday.'

Sindy was smirking and Barbie looked angry again.

'Tell us exactly what you heard,' said Teddy patiently.

'It was the children's parents. It seems they're moving to London – Mum, Dad and the children – and they're going to live in a flat, not a house any more,' Sindy told them. 'Katie's Mum said she and Carl must throw away the old toys or the ones they didn't play with any longer, because there won't be much room in the flat for extra toys.'

There was a long silence as the toys thought about the terrible news. Kite had been torn by Carl and Carl's Dad had promised to mend him but had forgotten to do so. Sammy the clockwork dog might still be useful for the new baby, but some of the old toys who were never played with nowadays were frightened and upset.

'They won't do it to us, will they, Teddy?' they asked fearfully, but Teddy wasn't sure.

'They're sure to get rid of some of us,' he said at last. 'Look at me with one ear hanging off and no growl any more.'

Everyone stared at him.

'But you belonged to Katie and Carl and the baby's Mum and her mother before that,' the other toys cried. 'They can't throw you in the bin, Teddy.'

'They can do what they like,' Teddy reminded them sadly. 'Whether we've comforted them and helped them or not, they can throw us on the rubbish heap any time, and don't you forget it!'

The other toys had a quiet respect for Teddy and his words made them sad and frightened.

'What a terrible way to treat old friends,' they said to each other.

As the time for the family move drew nearer, the children were told once again that old toys and books should be thrown away.

'I can't throw my friends in the bin,' protested Katie, and Carl, who was only 4, said, 'I won't throw any of my toys away.'

'But think how other children might enjoy them,' their mother said. 'If we find good homes for them, will you let them go then?'

'No,' replied Katie firmly.

'No,' echoed little Carl.

Teddy said very little to anyone nowadays. He sat in the toy cupboard by himself when Carl wasn't dragging him around and, when, in spite of Katie's and Carl's protests the old dolls were being placed in large cardboard boxes, Teddy still sat in the cupboard, absolutely certain that he would just go on the rubbish heap.

'Teddy, where will we go?' sobbed one of the dolls from inside the cardboard box.

'Oh, you'll go to a children's home or something like that,' Teddy told her, as cheerfully as he could.

There was no chattering among the toys once the lights were out, not these days.

The day before the move, a woman came from the local church to take the boxes of old toys and Teddy knew he should have managed to fall out of the cupboard and go with them. After all, he might have only one good ear and no growl, but some child somewhere might need him. Now it was too late and he'd have to join Kite and Sammy and the broken cars in the rubbish bin.

'Have I got everything?' asked the woman from the church.

'I'll just check,' the children's mother told her. 'I'll go upstairs and check the toy cupboard. The children may have left something up there.'

She ran upstairs and into the baby's room. She opened the toy cupboard and put her head inside it.

'Teddy!' she cried. 'What are you doing here all alone? You should be in the box with the others.'

'In the rubbish box or the box to go to the children's home?' Teddy asked himself gloomily. 'To think this lady was once a little girl and I loved her and she loved me.'

The children's mother was holding Teddy carefully.

'Ah, a teddy bear,' said the woman from the church. 'He's a bit old and worn, though,' she added doubtfully.

'Yes, he is, and he's staying here with us,' said the children's mother. 'Teddy has been with me all my life and he's much too valuable and important to give away. We've been searching through the luggage for him, but he must have fallen to the back of the cupboard.'

Teddy could hardly believe his ears. He was loved and wanted. They had been looking for him. He would always be a part of the family and need never worry again.

Barbie and Sindy are registered trade marks

The Prophet Muhammad and the lady with the rubbish

When the Prophet Muhammad lived in the Saudi Arabian city of Mecca he walked to the mosque every day along one of the city's main streets. He passed houses where women were brushing out rubbish and he always greeted them politely. One lady never answered the prophet's friendly greeting, however. She threw her rubbish all over Muhammad instead and then marched back into her house and slammed the door.

'Why don't you get your own back on that woman?' asked the prophet's friends angrily. 'She insults you every day.'

Muhammad did not believe that it would be right to deal with the woman's anger in this way.

'There must be a reason behind this,' he told his followers. 'Until I find it, I must be pleasant and patient with her.'

He could have walked on the other side of the street or he might have chosen another way to the mosque. The prophet continued to walk past the lady's house and to greet her politely but every day he had to brush away the rubbish she threw at him.

One day the woman was not there. Muhammad stared at the closed door anxiously.

'I hope she's alright,' he said.

His followers were amazed.

'Be thankful she isn't here for once,' they said, but the prophet smiled and said nothing.

After about a week, he decided he must find out where the woman was. He walked up to the front door and knocked. There was no reply and the prophet pushed the door gently. It swing open and he found the woman lying on a couch at the far end of the room. Muhammad went over to her at once. He found that she was weak from lack of food and water, and he gave her a drink and went to the people next door to borrow some food since there wasn't any in the house.

'Didn't you know she was ill?' he asked the woman's neighbours.

'Oh, she's so bad tempered we never bother with her,' they answered.

'Even so, we are supposed to help each other,' replied Muhammad quickly. 'I'm going to take care of her today and I'll visit every day, but I think you should call in tomorrow.'

One of Muhammad's friends had gone to find a doctor who arrived soon afterwards. The lady had taken some food and was able to explain what had happened.

'I slipped when I was standing on a chair to clean my walls,' she said. 'Then I felt sick and dizzy and I've been like this ever since.'

'She's hurt her back and had a bad shock,' the doctor said, 'but it isn't serious. She'll be alright but she shouldn't be left alone just yet.'

The prophet sat with the lady until evening and he found that she had not been in Mecca very long. Her husband had died and she had come to Mecca because she used to have relatives there. She found they had left the city a long time ago and she had been too frightened in the big city to make new friends.

'So I became lonely and bad tempered,' she said. 'I

didn't mean to be but I've forgotten how to be nice to people.'

When the neighbours went in the next day they found that the lady was friendly and grateful for their help. They arranged for others in the street to visit her as well and soon the lady had a lot of new friends.

Muhammad always had a special greeting from her after that and he was glad to know that the lady would not be lonely again. It might have been very different if the prophet had been angry with the lady for throwing rubbish at him or if he or his followers had thrown it back.

Changing the way we think

Class 1 always seemed to be in trouble. Bobby never shared his peanuts, and Tom was always unkind to other children in the class. Jamile told lies, and Jenny was rude to everyone. The list of all the naughty behaviour went on and on until Miss Doyle had an idea.

'Every day someone tells the children how naughty they are and they go on being bad', she thought. 'I wonder if it will work if I tell them how good they are for a change?'

She set to work and cut out 20 cardboard heads, one for each of the children, which she stuck on the wall. She wrote something good about each child on the head which had the child's name on it. Bobby's cardboard head said 'Bobby always shares his peanuts' (though he never did) and Jenny's said 'Jenny is always polite to everyone' (though she was not).

The next morning the children stared at the big cardboard heads.

'Miss has written something about us all,' said Tom. He looked at the words under his name: 'Tom helps all the younger children' it said.

At first, everyone laughed because they thought it was all a joke, but later that day they thought about the words. Tom had been just about to trip up a small boy, but he remembered the words 'Tom helps all the younger children' and he let the little boy go past safely.

Bobby was at the far end of the playground munching his peanuts, when he remembered Miss Doyle's words.

'You can have a nut, if you want,' he muttered to a surprised group not far from him.

Jenny and her friends were skipping in the Junior yard and heard the Infant School bell, but ignored it. When the Headteacher came to look for them, Jenny almost answered her back but said 'Sorry' instead, and Jamile later told the truth when she had accidentally upset someone's paints.

Of course, the children sometimes forgot, but the cardboard heads stayed on the wall to remind them that Miss Doyle knew they could change if they really tried. Later in the year some visitors came to the school. 'I think we'll let Class 1 show them round, because they are so pleasant and polite,' the Headteacher told the school at assembly, and Miss Doyle and her class smiled happily.

This is a true story. It really does make a difference if we think and say good things to each other. Everyone *can* make changes!

The echo

When Joanna was 3 years old she became very ill and her Mummy and Daddy gave her everything she asked for. She had more toys than anyone else in the street where she lived but she would not allow other children to play with them. If any of the children in the street had a toy which Joanna had not got she would ask her parents to buy one for her and they would do so.

'You are spoiling that child,' Grandma told Joanna's parents when she came to stay and saw her granddaugther snatch one of her dolls from a little girl who was visiting them. 'What will happen when she goes to school? She won't have any friends.'

'I don't want any friends,' said Joanna, who had overheard her grandmother. 'I don't need any.'

When she started school, the other children soon found that Joanna would not share anything with them. If she brought sweets to school she refused to share them and she boasted about her beautiful toys until the other children became angry and made fun of her. Whenever anyone in the class or in the street had a birthday party, Joanna would be left out, but she pretended she didn't mind.

'I told you this would happen,' said Grandma when she collected Joanna from school one day and heard the other children talking about her granddaughter.

'She'll grow out of it,' answered Joanna's mother.

'I don't think she will, not for a long time,' Grandma said. 'Look, why don't you let Joanna come to Switzerland with me in the summer? It will be company for me and since she hasn't any friends the summer holiday will seem long and boring for her.'

Joanna was excited about going to Switzerland even though she would rather have gone with Mummy and Daddy than Grandma, who was sometimes cross with her and wouldn't let her have her own way. She and her mother went to Preston, their nearest town and bought new clothes and shoes for Joanna's holiday.

Joanna and her grandmother got on together very well because Joanna did not dare ask Grandma to buy everything she wanted. They went on some beautiful trips through the mountains and Joanna began to look better every day.

'You look wonderful, Joanna,' Grandma said, pinching the little girl's rosy cheeks. 'I'm taking you on a very special trip today. We are going on a chair lift to one of the highest mountains. There's someone I'd like you to meet.'

'Not another child I hope,' replied Joanna who didn't think of herself as a child because she spent so much time with grown-ups.

'We'll see,' said Grandma mysteriously and an hour later she and Joanna were riding through the mountains in a chair lift. Joanna loved it and Grandma was glad to see her so happy but felt that her little granddaughter must learn a very important lesson.

They finally reached the top of the mountain which was famous for its wonderful echo. Now you and I know that

13

an echo is really our own voice coming back to us but Joanna didn't know this. When they arrived, a boy was cupping his hands and yelling into the mountains 'Hello!' His voice came back 'Hello! Hello! Hello!'

'There are people in the mountains shouting to that boy!' cried Joanna, as the boy shouted different things and his words came back to him.

'Why don't you try?' asked Grandma, as the boy moved away.

'Are they children or grown-ups?' asked Joanna.

'Children,' replied Grandma, and Joanna made a rude face and shouted, 'I don't like you!'

'Don't like you! Don't like you! Don't like you!' The voice came back.

Joanna glared at the other side of the mountain and shouted 'I hate you!' And the voice replied, 'I hate you! I hate you! I hate you!'

'Did you hear that?' Joanna was almost seething with rage. 'I won't show you my toys!'

'Won't show you my toys! Won't show you my toys! Won't show...'

Joanna was dancing up and down angrily. 'Shut up!' she yelled rudely and as the voice answered 'Shut up!' Grandma decided this had gone far enough.

'Joanna, why don't you shout something nice for a change?' she asked, and when Joanna had stopped crying Grandma said, 'Go on, Joanna. Tell that child you like them.'

'Won't,' answered Joanna sulkily, but she could see her Grandma meant her to do it, and she shouted 'I like you!'

'Like you, like you, like you!' came the reply. That was better.

'I'd like to be your friend,' shouted Joanna to her grandmother's surprise.

'Like to be your friend, like to be your friend,' came the voice.

'I'll show you my toys!' shouted Joanna, and to her delight the voice replied, 'Show you my toys, show you my toys!'

Joanna shouted a lot of nice things into the mountain and the voice did exactly the same since, as Grandma eventually explained, it was her own voice coming back to her.

'Though the other children at school and in the street are only nasty because you are nasty with them,' she said, 'if, when we get back you start being nice to them, you'll soon have lots of friends to play with and although you might not think it, you'll have lots of fun. You've had fun today ever since you started to shout nice things, haven't you? You thought it was another child in the mountains and you were pleased about it.'

Joanna was very quiet on the way back but Grandma made sure that, for the rest of the holiday, she took the little girl to places where there were children to see if she had really learnt how to talk to them. In the end, Joanna did make friends and enjoyed the holiday all the more because of it.

When she arrived home, she tried to be friendly to the other children in the street and at first they gave her a hard time and would not play with her, but in the end they began to include her in their games and by the time school began again she walked there with some of the new friends she had made.

It was a hard lesson for little Joanna to learn but she has a lot of friends now and would be the first to say to someone who hasn't, 'Are you being friendly to other people? If not, nothing will change until you do.'

Birth celebrations

The celebration of new life

- When I came into my family
- How babies are accepted into religious communities

The births of religious founders and leaders celebrated worldwide

- Stories and activities connected with the above
- Birth stories of Jesus, Muhammad, Moses, Krishna and Guru Nanak
- Making booklets on the birth of religious leaders

BIRTH CELEBRATIONS

Birthday celebrations

- Celebrating birthdays
- Growing older: life progress skills

LEARNING OBJECTIVES

- To be aware of the celebrations surrounding the birth of a new baby and the responses of family and friends.
- To learn about rituals surrounding the acceptance of a baby into a faith community.
- To recognise how birthdays celebrate the passage of time and how they mark the development of individual skills and abilities.
- To be acquainted with classical stories surrounding the births of several founders of world faiths.

STARTING POINTS

Cii

- Liaise with parents to bring in photographs of the children as babies and record important family events in which the children were involved. These might be christenings, naming ceremonies, weddings or birthdays. Divide the class into groups and ask them to place their photographs in chronological order. Spend time with each group in turn, helping pupils to identify the people in the photographs as well as events taking place.

- Invite two parents, one Christian and one Muslim, Hindu or Sikh, into the classroom with their babies. With the help of the guests, draw on the children's memories of excitement and wonder when a new baby is born in the family and the responses of relatives and friends when, for example, visiting the mother and new baby in hospital and at home.

- Invite the visiting parents to share experiences and information with the class concerning the welcoming of their new baby into the religious community (i.e. christenings and naming ceremonies). Photographs of times shared by the parents with their babies present will enable pupils to relate to events, dress, food (where displayed) more closely. Encourage children to ask questions themselves and write the names of the babies on the board, with useful information recorded beneath each name.

- Use posters and pictures of religious founders to introduce the stories surrounding the births of Jesus, Moses, Guru Nanak, Muhammad and Krishna. With the exception of the story of Muhammad's birth (as representations of the prophet as a baby are forbidden), stories may form the basis for a collage featuring all the characters and happenings we know of. Children may be able to write stories of events connected with their own births or early years.

- Examine photographs of any birthday parties to which children have recently been (including their own). Compare the photographs with those of the children at their first birthday celebrations. Introduce the birthday of Jesus by exploring with the children the excitement of Christmas and all that this celebration (including carols and songs) means to them. Where there are children of Muslim, Hindu, Sikh or Jewish faiths in the class, the birthday celebrations of their own founders or prophets can be included at this point.

- Learn and sing together the topic song, **Celebrate**, making sure that pupils realise how the coming of our religious founders gives us much to celebrate in our lives today.

THE CELEBRATION OF NEW LIFE

Area of study 1

C11 –14

Purpose
To help children to appreciate the excitement surrounding a baby's arrival in the family and the ways in which babies are accepted into the religious communities.

Activity 1: When I came into my family
A Give the children a fresh exercise book or make a book from pieces of sugar paper. Explain that these will be their special pictorial diaries which can be filled with photographs and their own writing about special events involving their personal histories. The events should be from the time they were babies and may include

photographs where family members and friends are taking part in a special occasion such as their christening or birthday celebrations. Every child should write his or her name on the cover of the book and on any photographs of themselves; they should also identify and label pictures of their relatives (see **Starting points**).

B Give out **Copymaster 11** (My family) which presents a diagram of a family tree. Pupils can fill in the names of the members of their family. They can also cut out and stick the diagram into their books when they have looked at each other's work and talked about their families together.

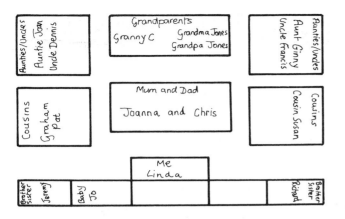

C Now put the photographs of the children as babies on the page of the diary following the family tree and record the name, age and possibly the weight of the child at the time of the photograph. Children can draw themselves at this time on **Copymaster 12** (Baby me) using a photograph they have on which to base their picture. Place the completed copymaster in their diary after the photographs.

D Talk with the children about the arrival of a new baby and write words on the board which the children might give to describe their feelings at this time. Such words as 'happy', 'excited', 'jealous' should all be carefully explored, and the children fully encouraged to express their true feelings, however negative they may be.

Ask the children what happens when a new baby is born in the home of a relative or friend. Suggest that everyone wants to see the new baby, to give him or her a special welcome and take a present. Write these examples down on the blackboard and then ask the children to write a short description about what they might do when they heard the exciting news of a baby's birth.

Activity 2: How babies are accepted into religious communities

A Tell the children they are all going to learn about how babies are accepted into their religious communities, not only at home but also in their local place of worship to where they will be going from an early age.

B Prepare a range of flashcards and read the story **Jo-Jo's christening** (p. 22), explaining that this is a story about a baby girl who was accepted into her Christian community and that pupils must listen to the story carefully because afterwards you will be asking them what happened.

After discussing the story, show the children the flashcards containing important words to do with the christening, such as 'vicar', 'font', 'water', 'godparent', and so on, and ask them what each means.

C Tell the children that they are going on a special trip to take part in a christening ceremony and arrange this with the local vicar, asking for his help in organising a mock ceremony for the class.

In the classroom, divide the children into 'family' groups of 'parents' and 'godparents', etc., using dolls for the 'babies'. Set out for the church reverently, keeping together in the family groups. At the church, the vicar, after welcoming the 'christening parties' will explain the service of infant baptism as simply as possible, allowing 'godparents' to participate fully and baptising each 'baby' in turn.

The return journey should be as reverent as the outward one and a small party can be held in the classroom to celebrate the occasion afterwards. Photographs taken of each family group can be exhibited in the classroom or children might include these in their diaries.

✓ Distribute **Copymaster 13** (Celebration day!). Discuss with the children all they remember of the christening ceremony and how they felt about it, then ask them to record what they learnt from their visit on the copymaster. In the top six boxes there are labelled pictures of significant events, items or people. Children can use these as a guide to fill in the blanks in the lower six boxes. All the boxes can then be cut out and arranged on a large sheet of black sugar paper in the form of a story with decorated pictures in the right order and matching sentences placed underneath.

D Read the story **Ranjit is named** (p. 23). Tell the children beforehand that the story describes a different sort of naming ceremony – one that happens at a Hindu temple. Afterwards, discuss the differences between the two ceremonies (for example, the priest named the baby in the Christian baptism, whereas in the story Mandeep's father announced the name of her baby brother).

Use **Copymaster 14** (Church or temple?) to recognise the eight objects and people found in a church and a temple at a baptism and naming ceremony. The children should write 'C' or 'T' in the boxes provided.

E If possible, visit a Sikh gurdwara where a Sikh elder or granthi may be willing to explain the naming ceremony to the children. Similarly, a local Hindu temple education officer might be able to visit the school and assist the children with the acting out of a Hindu naming ceremony.

On all occasions, photographs will remind the children of those who participated, the events which occurred and the clothes that participants wore.

F Show the class 'A Surprise Birth', Programme One of the ITV Schools RE series *Coming Together*. Draw the children's attention to the shared meal which would take place after the naming ceremony in a Sikh community.

Investigate what kinds of foods are eaten by people of the Christian, Sikh and Hindu faiths when they celebrate special occasions together. If there is time, look at other 'celebration food' eaten by people of different faiths. Draw simple pencil and crayon sketches of this food and name it.

Area of study 2

BIRTHDAY CELEBRATIONS

C15 –17

Purpose
To look at what is involved in birthday celebration and examine how children have changed and developed as each birthday has passed.

Activity 1: Celebrating birthdays
A Sit the children informally and read them the short story **A birthday party** (p. 23). Afterwards, talk about what was mentioned in the story that made the party a special occasion, one of fun and celebration for everyone. Was it the food (the special birthday cake), the surprises or the co-operation of all participants that made the party enjoyable?

B Tell the children you are all going to plan a special birthday party for several children in the class whose birthdays occur at around the same time. Let all pupils participate fully in the planning of the activities for this celebration.

C Provide children with a variety of materials and make birthday cards for those whose birthdays are to be celebrated. These cards could be drawn and coloured in with crayons or paints. Alternatively, make collage cards with a three-dimensional effect incorporating number 'badges', a birthday cake, a girl or boy in birthday clothes, and so on.

D Use **Copymaster 15** (Our party) to send invitations from the class to parents, governors, lunchtime supervisors and other people who help in school, making sure that the invitations are attractive and colourful and that the writing is neat and clear.

E Organise the classroom for your party. **Copymaster 16** (My classroom party plan) provides a key of symbols representing four main party areas. Ask pupils to select a different colour for each symbol, colour in the key appropriately, then devise a simple classroom plan in the space provided, using the symbols accordingly. Explain that they may wish to use a symbol more than once. Take the children's work into consideration when arranging the classroom.

To add atmosphere, make decorations for the classroom walls and ceiling, such as brightly coloured streamers.

badge made out of stiff card with number made from foil or glittered

glittered candle flames

candles (coloured card)

textured white paint for icing

cake stand (sugar paper)

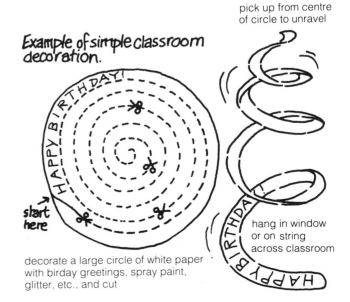

Example of simple classroom decoration.

pick up from centre of circle to unravel

start here

decorate a large circle of white paper with birday greetings, spray paint, glitter, etc., and cut

hang in window or on string across classroom

Make posters saying 'Welcome to our celebration!' and 'Celebrate with us!' reminding the children that they are involved in the planning of a celebration.

F Ask the class to tell you what are the three main 'ingredients' to a successful celebration (i.e. music, games and food) and invite them to make their own choices for each, paying particular attention to the wishes of those whose birthdays are being celebrated.

Pupils can select a range of music to which the whole class will enjoy listening, incorporating as many different styles as possible to represent the cultures of class members: for example, reggae, rock, Asian, Soul, etc.

Then make a list of well-known games and devise some original ones. Set up and present aspects of celebration from several faiths, using information gathered in this topic.

Finally, the children can select a variety of foods from different cultures. Remind them of the story **A birthday party**.

G After all this preparation, children can be given various jobs at the time of the party to make it a success: for example, as hosts to welcome guests at the classroom door; as food monitors to serve the food and keep the tables tidy; as games organisers to assist in the setting up of the games and the allocation of teams, and so on.

H Choose a time during the course of the party when groups of children are receptive to a quieter time together. Ask them what they are enjoying most about the celebration. Is it the games, the food, or being happy together because they had all helped out?

19

Activity 2: Growing older every year

Soon after the party other aspects of birthdays, such as marking the passing of time and acquiring greater skills, can be explored. Note with the children the tasks they are able to perform now but could not one year ago. What things do they expect to be able to do for themselves in 12 months' time?

✓ Use **Copymaster 17** (When did I...?) to measure how much more the children can do now than in previous years. The children can use a different colour for each time span and visualise how their skills have developed since they were very young. A note could be sent home with the copymaster asking for parents' co-operation:

Dear Parent

We are doing a survey in class of your child's life progress skills from years 1 to 5. Please could you help us by filling in the information on the enclosed sheet with your child present.

The results of the survey can be presented in the form of a bar graph.

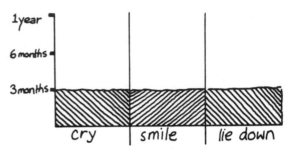

| Area of study 3 | **BIRTHS OF RELIGIOUS FOUNDERS** | C18 –20 |

Purpose

To be aware of the stories connected with the births of religious founders, that are celebrated all over the world.

Activity 1: Christ is with us

A Use **Copymaster 18** (My birth factsheet) to remind the children of their arrival into the world and make a record of the important facts about themselves when they were born.

B Give out newspapers and magazines containing photographs of when royal babies are born. Discuss why such events are publicly announced in the newspapers and on television.

C Show the children a globe or world map and point out the position of Israel. Tell them that Bethlehem in that country is an important place as it was where the baby Jesus was born 2 000 years ago. Suggest that pupils create a 'Bethlehem collage' of houses, a synagogue, landscape features, an inn, a stable, etc., to set the scene for the Nativity story. Simple strips of brown paper can be painted and screwed up to give the appearance of a rocky surface (cross-reference **Sacred books**, p. 66).

D Show the first part of 'A Surprise Birth', Programme One of the ITV Schools RE series *Coming Together*, to help convey the Christmas atmosphere, then read the story **A Christmas baby** (p. 23). On a large sheet of paper, write down as many words to describe Christmas celebrations as the children can think of and ask them to draw small diagrams illustrating each one.

E Divide the class into groups so that each group can role-play part of the Christmas story. Dress in costumes, usually available in schools for Nativity plays, or, alternatively, use sheets, dressing gowns and striped towels.

A Bethlehem collage

Activity 2: Muhammad and Mecca

A Discuss journeys with the children and list the items which might be taken if they were to make a long journey abroad.

B Invite a member of the local Muslim community who has been on a pilgrimage to Mecca. Ask the visitor to show the children the two pieces of white cloth that he or she wore on their visit and, with the help of a videotape showing thousands of people in Mecca, the visitor could explain what Mecca is like and why he or she went there.

C Remind the children that their visitor is a Muslim, a member of the faith known as Islam, and that he or she worships one God known as Allah. Use flashcards showing the words, 'Muslim', 'Mecca', 'Pilgrimage', 'Muhammad', 'Allah', etc. to reinforce elements of the Islamic faith.

D Reconstruct the visitor's journey to Mecca from the moment they left their home in Britain to their dawn prayers at Jeddah airport and their journey to Mecca itself from that point. Remind the children that Mecca would be extremely hot.

E Read the story **The Prophet Muhammad's birth** (p. 24) to the children and discuss the climate and conditions of Mecca and the surrounding desert region. Children can then create a desert scene and tents of the Bedouin tribes from sugar paper and felt. Although the Prophet Muhammad as a baby cannot be represented, the scene could include tribal women taking their new foster children back to their desert homes.

Activity 3: Moses the infant

A Consult a globe and travel brochures to ascertain the present route to Egypt and obtain an old map, showing the children the River Nile and the area called Goshen where the Israelite slaves were housed.

B Show the class a 'Moses basket'. Tell them what it is called and ask them if they know why this type of basket has this special name. Explain that they are going to hear the story of the birth of Moses and they will soon find out. Read **The birth of Moses** (p. 24).

A Moses basket

C Act the story of Moses' adoption by Pharaoh's daughter.

D Show the children the second part of 'Part of the Family', the Jewish programme from the ITV Schools RE series *Coming Together*, which tells of the story of Moses and his eventual role of Deliverer and the founder of the religion of Judaism.

Activity 4: Who is Krishna?

A Show the children a large picture and statue of Krishna. Explain to them that Krishna is an important god in the Hindu faith and that he is worshipped by thousands of people in India and in Britain.

B Play a tape of Indian music and light incense sticks to help to create atmosphere. Gather the children into a circle and tell them the story of **Krishna's birth** (p. 25).

C Visit a Hindu temple which has a Krishna shrine and ask someone from the temple's Education Department to tell the children more about Krishna as a baby.

Activity 5: Baby Nanak

A Introduce the birth story of Guru Nanak by showing the children slides of the temple at Amritsar and of Sikhs wearing traditional dress. Explain that

Guru Nanak was the founder of, or person who began, the Sikh faith which led to the building of this beautiful temple and the adoption of the Sikh uniform.

B Take the children on an imaginary journey back to the fifteenth century to a small village in north-west India known as Talwandi, a name which really means 'white' because it was not far from a desert and was often covered in sand.

Tell the children that at that time a baby was born to the wife of a village accountant called Kalu, and they are going to hear the story of what happens after Kalu is told by a servant that he has a son. Read the story, **The**

birth of Guru Nanak (p. 25), to find out what happens next.

C After the story, show the children pictures of Guru Nanak from the Sikh histories. They can draw their own pictures of the baby Nanak, Kalu and the priest.

D Let the children pretend to be Nanaki, the baby's sister. Ask them to write a brief description of what she would tell her friends about her baby brother.

Activity 6: Four special births

A Recap with the children on the main facts they have learnt about the births of Jesus, Moses, Guru Nanak and Krishna and use **Copymasters 19** and **20** (Four special births 1 and 2) to make four fold-up booklets about the four special births. Children fill in the correct words in each section. The following words should be written on the board for pupils to read aloud and then select and copy on to the copymasters:

- Jesus – manger, stable
- Moses – waterproof basket, River Nile
- Nanak – cradle, bedroom
- Krishna – basket, dungeon.

All sections can be coloured in, cut out and folded. A suitable front cover should be designed while the pictures of the stable, River Nile, bedroom and dungeon form the back cover of the booklets when folded.

TOPIC STORIES

Jo-Jo's christening

Kayleigh sat at the front of the church with her two Grans and Grandpas and watched her mother and father go to the font where Father John was waiting to christen baby Jo-Jo. Aunty Lizzie, one of Jo-Jo's godmothers, was carrying the baby and Aunty Ruth, the second godmother and Uncle Garry, Jo-Jo's godfather, were walking on either side of Aunty Lizzie. Father John held out his arms for the baby and asked her name.

'Jodie Elizabeth,' said Aunty Lizzie proudly.

'Her name's Jo-Jo,' said Kayleigh loudly and Grandpa whispered, 'No. Jo-Jo is our pet name for her. She has to use her real name when she is christened.'

Father John was holding little Jo-Jo carefully and with his free hand he scooped some water from the font and made the sign of the cross on the baby's forehead.

'Jodie Elizabeth, I baptise you in the name of the Father and of the Son and of the Holy Spirit, Amen,' said Father John clearly. Jo-Jo started to cry. Kayleigh pushed past Grandpa and ran to the font.

'Don't cry, Jo-Jo, I'm here,' she said and her Daddy laughed and caught her hand.

'Stay with me,' he whispered. 'Jo-Jo will be alright.'

Aunty Ruth now had Jo-Jo. A few minutes ago she, Aunty Lizzie, Uncle Garry and Kayleigh's parents had all promised to bring up Jo-Jo in the Christian faith, making promises to God for her until Jo-Jo could make those promises for herself.

When they were walking to the church hall where the christening party was to be held, Kayleigh caught up with her Grandpa.

'Did I get christened like that?' she asked.

'You certainly did,' he answered, smiling at her. 'And there was a big party afterwards, just as we are going to have now.'

Ranjit is named

Mandeep was so excited that she couldn't keep still. It was a Sunday morning in Narenler and her baby brother was to be taken to the temple for his naming ceremony.

Mandeep's grandparents had come for the occasion, her mother's parents from India and her father's from Birmingham. They lived only two blocks from the Sikh temple in Preston, Lancashire, and the entire family and all their friends walked to the temple, Mandeep's mother carrying the baby and Mandeep holding her father's hand.

When they reached the temple everyone took off their shoes and placed them in the cloakrooms to the left of the entrance. All the women covered their heads with silk scarves and the men not wearing turbans fastened handkerchiefs on their heads.

There were a number of worshippers in the prayer hall already and the naming party went to the front of the temple, the men and women separating so that the men were on the left and the women on the right. Everyone went to the raised platform in turn, bowing their heads to the ground before the Guru Granth Sahib, the Sikh holy book, which was above them under a large canopy.

The granthi, or reader, opened the book and read the first hymn on the left-hand page. The first word began with the letter 'R'. Mandeep's father stood to face his family and the congregation.

'We shall call the baby "Ranjit",' he said, speaking in Punjabi. 'Let the congregation agree.'

The congregation did agree. They replied 'Sat Sri Akal' meaning 'Truth is Eternal' as a welcome to baby Ranjit, who was now a member of the Sikh community.

A birthday party

Class 2 were having a birthday party. Three children, Timmy, Katie and Jayant, had their sixth birthdays in the same week and Miss Andrews their teacher thought they should share their party and make it a big celebration.

The school cooks made a special birthday cake with the children's names written on it in pink, blue and green icing. Timmy's mother brought some sandwiches and home-made cakes. Katie's mother provided ice-cream and biscuits for the whole class and Jayant's mother made bhajis and Indian sweets for everyone to share.

All the children had a small parcel to take home. Some of the girls and boys opened these as soon as they left the school and found they each had been given a piece of birthday cake, biscuits and some brightly coloured Indian sweets.

A Christmas baby

'Are you warm enough, Mary?' asked Joseph anxiously. It was a cold night and they still had a long way to go before they saw the lights of Bethlehem.

'Yes, thank you. This cloak is warm,' answered Mary, though she didn't look warm as she sat patiently on the donkey's back.

'We'll soon be there now,' Joseph told her soothingly. 'Then we'll soon be comfortable again.'

'Do you think it will be hard to find a room?' asked Mary. 'After all, we aren't going to be there until nightfall.'

'Oh, there is always room for latecomers,' replied Joseph but this had been worrying him too. They had travelled a long way and with the baby due to arrive at any time they had to go slowly.

Darkness was falling now and the road to Bethlehem seemed to be narrower in the half light. Joseph took the donkey's bridle and led the little animal around the bend in the road. Then he stopped so suddenly that Mary might have fallen from the donkey if Joseph had not put out his free hand to steady her.

'What is it, Joseph?' cried Mary.

'It is Bethlehem – just down there in the hollow,' answered Joseph joyfully. 'We'll be there in no time at all now.'

They stopped at the first inn a few minutes later. There were sounds of laughter and chatter from inside but the innkeeper's pleasant face changed when they asked for a room.

'At this hour? We've been full since midday,' he told them. 'Try further on.'

Mary and Joseph thanked the innkeeper and tried the next inn, a large one on the main road.

'Sorry, we're full.' The innkeeper hardly bothered to open the door.

'But my wife's having a baby,' Joseph told him.

'Well, then, you should have left her at home. We've been full for hours now. Goodnight.' The innkeeper shut the door firmly.

'I was afraid of this,' whispered Mary, who was feeling very tired and cold.

The next inns were obviously full. They were in darkness and Joseph had no wish to wake everyone.

'There's one more – a small one on the other side of town,' he told Mary. 'It's been there for years. I'm sure they'll take us on.'

When they reached the small building there was only a faint light showing which must have been out in the courtyard beyond the inn itself. Joseph knocked on the inn door and after a few moments it opened.

'Yes?' The landlord was rubbing his eyes as if he had just woken up.

'Have you a room to spare, please?' asked Joseph, wearily.

'No, I'm afraid we haven't,' replied the landlord. 'You are a bit late, you know.'

'Oh, please, anywhere will do,' Joseph pleaded. 'My wife's baby will soon be here and we are worn out.'

'I'm sorry –' began the innkeeper. He was about to close the door but a voice inside the inn stopped him.

'There aren't any rooms,' he said, turning back to Joseph. 'But my wife tells me the stable is clean. You'd have to sleep with the animals, but it's better than open fields.'

'Anything, anything. We'll be glad of it.' Joseph was helping Mary from the donkey.

Following the landlord through the inn to the courtyard beyond, Mary felt deeply thankful for the kindness of the innkeeper and his wife. They were soon in the warm stable and the landlord was putting fresh straw on the floor for them. The weary donkey was brought in too and given fresh hay to munch.

The innkeeper and his wife were woken again in the early hours of the morning. Three shepherds were at the door and they told the surprised innkeeper that the Saviour of the World had been born in the inn stable.

'What are you talking about?' asked the innkeeper.

'Look – there's a big star in the sky and it is right over your stable.' One of the shepherds pointed upwards and the innkeeper could not believe his eyes. He hurried into the courtyard followed by the shepherds and knocked softly on the stable door.

Joseph opened the stable door, smiling at the visitors, a finger on his lips to tell them to be quiet. They crept into the stable and there, in a manger lay a baby – the baby Jesus, the Saviour of the World.

The Prophet Muhammad's birth

In the year 570 a baby boy called Muhammad was born in Mecca in Saudi Arabia. Muhammad's father was a brave soldier and he died defending the city of Mecca shortly before his son's birth. Therefore, the new baby lived at first with his mother and grandparents.

Mecca was a hot and dirty city in those days. It was not a healthy place for new babies and most parents paid for their children to be taken into the desert to live with foster parents until they were 4 years old.

Every day, women came to Mecca from the desert to take the new babies. No one wanted Muhammad because his father was dead and his mother could not afford to pay very much money. In the end, just when the baby's mother thought she would have to keep him in Mecca, a foster mother came forward. She was poor, but she loved children and she wanted very much to take Muhammad, even though his mother would not be able to give her much money for his keep.

Muhammad loved his foster mother and he never forgot her. He became a famous ruler, won many battles and was the last and greatest prophet of the Muslim faith, Islam. He was kind, loving and trustworthy and cared for his foster mother all her life, taking her to live with his family when she became too old to look after herself.

The birth of Moses

The King of Egypt had given a cruel order to his soldiers. They were to go to a part of Egypt called Goshen where all the Israelites lived and they were to take all the newly-born baby boys and throw them into the River Nile. The King was afraid that too many baby boys were being born to the Israelites and felt that one day, if Egypt should be attacked by another country, the Israelites would join the enemy and fight against Egypt.

One mother was determined to save her son. She hid him for as long as she could but when the baby grew too big to hide any longer his mother had an idea. She took a basket, painted it with tar inside and out to make it waterproof and then, wrapping her baby warmly in a shawl she placed him carefully in the basket. All the Israelites had to work as slaves for the King of Egypt and there was no one watching when the brave woman, taking her little daughter with her, carried the basket to the River Nile.

'Are you going to put our baby in the river, Mother?' asked Miriam, the baby's sister, in surprise.

'No, of course not,' answered her mother.

She placed the basket in the tall grass by the riverbank.

'Now I want you to stay here and watch him carefully,' she told Miriam and walked quickly away before the little girl could argue.

Miriam stood obediently by the trees not far from the river. She wondered how long it would be before her baby brother started to cry.

'And then what do I do?' she wondered to herself.

Suddenly Miriam heard laughter from the riverbank. A group of young girls ran down to wade into the water throwing a large brightly coloured ball to each other.

'It's the Princess,' Miriam thought, watching one of the young girls who was dressed in beautiful clothes. 'What will I do if they wake the baby?'

The ball arrived in the long grass with a loud plop and the baby in the basket began to cry loudly.

'Who made that noise?' cried the Princess, looking at her friends accusingly.

'None of us did, Princess. It came from over there.' One of them pointed to the bank and the Princess hurried forward, splashing through the water.

'Look!' she shouted. 'It's a basket and the noise is coming from inside it.'

At first the other girls were frightened but the Princess had already reached the basket and she was opening it carefully.

24

'It's a baby,' she cried and as the other girls crowded round her she lifted the little boy into her arms and cuddled him lovingly.

'Your Highness, it is an Israelite child,' said one of the Princess' friends, as she noticed the Israelite shawl.

'Yes, I know that,' replied the King's daughter. 'But he belongs to me now. I shall call him Moses. That means "drawn from the water".'

'But, how can you look after him?' one of the young girls asked. 'Your father will know he's an Israelite.'

'I shall find a nurse for him,' said the Princess.

Miriam, listening behind the trees, dared to run forward from her hiding place.

'I can find you a nurse, your Highness,' she said, curtseying to the King's daughter.

The Princess looked at her and nodded.

'Fetch me a nurse now,' she ordered and Miriam ran home at once.

A few minutes later, the Princess was handing the baby back to his own mother.

'Look after him for five years and then bring him to me at the palace,' she said. 'You will be paid well.'

As Miriam and her mother went joyfully away, little Moses safely in his mother's arms, one of the Princess' friends looked after them.

'You know, Princess, that's probably the child's own mother,' she said.

'Yes, of course it is,' replied the Princess calmly. 'Who can look after a child better than his own mother?'

Five years later Moses, the Israelite child, became Prince Moses, adopted son of the King's daughter.

Krishna's birth

Lord Krishna, one of the Hindu gods, was born on a dark and stormy night in the dungeons of a gloomy prison. His parents were the rightful rulers but they had been put in prison by the wicked King Kans who now ruled the country.

King Kans had been told that one of his brother's children would kill him, so every time his sister-in-law gave birth to a baby, the King rushed to the palace dungeons and murdered the child.

Krishna was the eighth child and on the night of his birth there was such a bad storm that the King in his bedroom above the dungeons did not hear the cries of a new baby.

As soon as Krishna was born, his father put the baby in a basket. The prison doors opened for him and he walked out of the palace into the night. Krishna's father took him many miles away to the home of a cowherd, whose wife had just had a baby girl. The two children were exchanged and the little girl was taken back to the palace where King Kans killed her.

The King soon realised that the real child of his brother and sister-in-law had managed to escape, but although he did his best to find Krishna, no one could tell him anything about the missing child.

Krishna was loved by everyone. Years later he removed King Kans from his throne and put his parents, the rightful King and Queen, in King Kans' place. They ruled for many years.

The birth of Guru Nanak

'That is wonderful!' cried Kalu, when the servant told him. 'How is my wife?'

'She is doing well, Sir,' answered the servant. 'But she would like you to hurry home to see the baby.'

'I'll be home soon,' promised Kalu. 'Tell my wife that.'

When Kalu arrived home, he was surprised to see Nanaki, his little girl, sitting on the doorstep.

'What's wrong, Nanaki?' asked Kalu, putting his arm around the little girl. 'Don't you like your new brother?'

'I love him,' answered Nanaki, 'but the nurse is saying funny things about him.'

'What kind of things?' asked Kalu, sharply.

'She says that when the baby was born he laughed loudly like a grown-up person at a party,' said Nanaki. 'But he couldn't do that, could he, because he's only a baby.'

'Of course he couldn't do anything like that,' answered Kalu. 'Wait here. I'll go in to see your mother and the baby. Is he like you?'

'Yes, he is,' said Nanaki proudly and Kalu laughed as he went into the house.

Tripta, his wife, was lying in bed with the cradle beside her. Kalu looked into the cradle at once.

'He seems just an ordinary baby to me,' he told Tripta. 'You didn't hear him laugh, did you?'

'No, I didn't and I'm sure the nurse didn't, either,' said Tripta. 'We don't want her telling strange tales.'

Nurse Davlatan told Kalu she had definitely heard the baby laugh loudly like a grown-up person at a party.

'You must have imagined it,' said Kalu sternly. 'No baby could do that.'

Mr Hardial, the village priest, called to see the new baby, but Tripta said the child should stay in his cradle because it was a cold day and she didn't want him to be ill.

'I've been hearing some rumours about your baby,' the priest told Kalu.

'It's the nurse. She thought she heard the child laugh loudly like a grown man at a party,' said Kalu. 'She must have told the whole village.'

'I'd better see her,' said Mr Hardial.

'Tell me,' the priest said to the nurse 'when this child was born, did he laugh loudly like a grown man?'

'He did, Sir,' answered the nurse. 'He laughed in a deep voice and I was really frightened.'

'Please, Kalu, let me see the child,' said the priest and the baby, still in his swaddling clothes, was brought to Mr Hardial.

As soon as the priest saw the baby he turned to Kalu.

'This child will be known all over the world,' he said. 'He will be one of the world's great leaders, and everyone will listen to him.'

Kalu could not believe it and he was not pleased with the priest.

'My son is a Hindu and he will be either an accountant like me or a farmer,' he said.

Food

Our food

- Food we eat and where it comes from
- Food of different cultures

Celebration food

- Looking at celebration food

FOOD

Hunger

- Why are some people hungry?
- What can we do to help provide food?

Greed

- Feeling too full
- How to stay healthy

LEARNING OBJECTIVES

- To appreciate human and animal dependence upon the earth's resources and to be familiar with expressions of gratitude.
- To be aware of rules and customs governing the lives of others.
- To acquire knowledge of religious customs, traditions and festivals in relation to food preparation and consumption.
- To be aware of different ways of showing care and concern.
- To associate places of worship with ceremonies marking the seasons.
- To learn how different foods are used in special ways and for special occasions.

STARTING POINTS

Ciii

- Before the session prepare samples of different food. These should ideally be in small identical dishes so that the food is the focus of the children's attention. Each food sample should be chosen to show contrast in colour and care should be taken to present food with a wide variety of taste. Examples of this could be foods with which children are familiar – vegetables, yogurt, fruit, baked beans, burgers – to contrast with other foods that they might not eat regularly such as pilau rice, pasta shells, tuna fish and pizza.

Gathered informally around a large table where the food is on display, ask the children to recognise the samples and as they do so write down the names of each food on a name card (like a place setting card) and put the cards in front of each food sample.

- Show pupils colourful pictures of food from magazines or books. Ask them where they think this food comes from. Bring tins and packets of food into school and ask the children to examine the labels. What does the label tell them? Does the food come from the address on the label or somewhere else? Contrast, for instance, a packet of Cheddar cheese produced in this country and a packet of rice grown in India.

Children can create collages of foods and their countries of origin. This would be a good opportunity to work in small groups and to prepare pupils for the activities in Area of Study 1.

- Write a list of foods the children like on the blackboard. Ask the children to give examples of as many different foods as they can think of from other countries. Write the name of the country by the food.

- Remind the children of when they were looking at pictures of themselves and their expressions when they

were finding out about Big Me and Little Me. Ask them to draw two portraits of themselves. The first picture should show the child looking happy, holding a plate piled high with food. The second picture should show the child looking miserable, holding a plate with no food on it. Ask the children to think carefully about their expression in both pictures. How do they feel in each portrait? Why? Write down their suggestions in two columns on the board or large sheet of paper.

☺ Full plate	☹ Empty plate
happy	miserable
content	hopeless
grateful	angry
pleased	sad
excited	deprived
satisfied	gloomy

- Ask the children to think about as many people as they can who give them food every day. They can write these names down. Ask them if they ever say 'thank you' to these people for providing them with food.

- Play the topic song, **Food, food, food!**, and ask which parts sound happy and which sound sad: pick out the happy and sad words and list them in two columns on the board. Now learn and sing the song together.

OUR FOOD

Area of study 1

C21 –25

Purpose
To look at food and where it comes from and to study the food of different cultures.

Activity 1: The food we eat and where it comes from
A Take the children over to the samples of food arranged on the table that were looked at in **Starting**

points. Revise the names of the items and discuss the colour and shape of the food with them. Point out that the food in front of them is only a very small sample of different types of food that exist in our world and that we are lucky to have such a wide variety to choose from to eat. Say that you are all going to find out where this food comes from.

B Put up a large world map on the classroom wall. Revise with the children where different countries are. Ask them to draw and cut out pictures of food made here in our own country and food brought into this country to be eaten. Give each child a picture to draw, colour and cut out. Examples might be a bottle or carton of milk, eggs, cheese, tomatoes, fish, sausages, apples, a bar of chocolate, spaghetti or pasta shells, a bowl of rice, coffee beans, a steaming pot of tea, bananas, mangoes, sugar and so on.

Copymaster 21 (Food!) shows illustrations of different types of food we can eat. The children have to recognise the pictures and fill in the correct word underneath using the printed words at the bottom of the copymaster to help them. They can cut out the pictures and stick them on to the world map with your guidance. Explain that many foods make long journeys from all over the world in order to reach our supermarket shelves.

C The children can make posters showing these different foods and the country from which the food has come.

Now distribute **Copymaster 22** (Which country?). The children should fill in the chart by drawing a picture of each food, writing down the name of the country or countries from where it comes, and the climate of the countries suitable for growing the food (for example, hot, dry, wet, warm).

D Show the children a bottle or carton of milk. Explain to them that milk is an essential food containing vitamins which are necessary for our growth and health: this is why as babies we relied upon milk as our only source of food. Ask the children if they know where milk comes from.

E Use **Copymaster 23** (Milk's journey) showing the journey of milk from the cow to the supermarket shelf. Discuss what happens to produce the milk in the bottle or carton by looking at the pictures. Pupils can colour

the pictures in and write the appropriate words beneath them. Ask them to follow the journey with their finger or draw over the route with a coloured pencil or felt-tip pen. They can then stick the sheet into their workbooks and write a few sentences about how milk eventually arrives on the supermarket shelf.

Contrast this example of food produced in our country with an example of food from a foreign country. This might be, for instance, bananas or chocolate. Talk them through the journey with the aid of prepared pictures and ask them if they can tell you what happens next by looking at the sequence shown.

F Provide the children with a large selection of recipe books full of colourful photographs. Point out to them that the foods they have just been learning about can be used in various ways to make delicious meals. Show them the bottle or carton of milk again and ask them to think of various ways milk is used when making other food – suggest cream and yogurt. Look at a bunch of bananas with them and ask them what they could make with them – cake, biscuits, ice-cream, etc. Show them a bar of chocolate and then a packet of chocolate biscuits, a chocolate cake, a jar of chocolate spread, a sachet of hot chocolate drink. Say these are all examples of food in which chocolate is found in different forms.

G Ask the children to recognise the shape of foods given on **Copymaster 24** (Food shapes). Revise with them the shapes written at the bottom of the pictures by drawing sketches on the board. The children then have to look at the copymaster again and match the word shape with the correct picture. In the lower section, the children can draw some more pictures of food and write down their corresponding shapes.

H Have on hand a range of cook books and invite the children to make recipe cards for banana milkshake, chocolate crispy cakes and yogurt. Under your supervision, the children can make the foods and enjoy a feast together!

☐I☐ Ask the children to play the 'Which shop?' game. Divide them into small groups and give each group the title of a food shop such as 'chip shop', 'greengrocer', 'supermarket', 'baker', 'butcher', and so on. Tell each group they must keep the title of the shop a secret. Then gather the children together and tell them they are going to watch each group mime the activities in the shop and the way the food is handled. Class members have to guess what type of shop it is, what is sold there and what is happening.

Activity 2: Food of different cultures

☐A☐ Focus on the food rice with the children. Sit them informally and show them a packet of rice. Do they know where the rice comes from? Point on the world map to China, the Far East and the USA. Ask a few able children to put pictures of rice on the world map in the right places. If possible, show the class pictures of how rice is grown and harvested.

☐B☐ Have samples of different types of rice on show, such as packets of different grains, rice in a ready meal packet with a curry sauce, an opened tin of rice pudding, a packet of Rice Krispies. Ask the children which rice food they would eat and why.

Explain to the children that rice is a food eaten by people of different cultures. Show them again the ready meal of curry and rice and point out that the delicate taste of the rice compliments the hot, strong flavour of the curry and this meal is particularly enjoyed by Indian people.

☐C☐ Have samples on show of other foods eaten by people from a variety of cultures. Focus on bread and meat, two universal foods. Display different types of bread such as a sandwich loaf, naan bread, pitta bread, chapatti and a French stick. Discuss with the children who tends to eat each type: for example, Muslim people enjoy chapattis. Then show the children small samples of minced beef, diced pork, slices of salami and pieces of chicken and talk about the people who would eat these meats and those people who, because of their cultural and religious beliefs, would not eat some of the foods. For example, point out that Hindus do not eat beef

because they believe a cow is sacred and Jewish people do not eat pork because they believe that pigs are unclean. Say that for these reasons the food human beings eat varies between cultures.

☐D☐ Write the word 'vegetarian' on the board and ask the children if they know its meaning. Explain to them that vegetarians do not eat meat for personal or religious reasons but choose to eat a diet based upon cereals, dairy products, pasta, rice, fruit and vegetables.

☐E☐ Finish by playing the 'tasting game' with the children. Divide them into groups and invite them to take it in turns to taste a different food sample looked at and talked about by everyone earlier on. Make sure all foods vary in taste and texture (for example, they could taste chocolate, milk, banana, lemon, savoury spread, pasta, pizza). This game is done under blindfold conditions.

✓ **Copymaster 25** (Taste it!) allows children to record whether they recognised the food by its taste and texture. They should fill in the columns correctly for each food given. Afterwards the children can offer their own ideas for food taste recognition.

Discuss the results as a class and remind the children that although we all recognise and enjoy certain sweet or salty foods we must not eat too many as this will make us unhealthy.

29

Purpose

To explore what it feels like to be constantly hungry and what can be done to help those who suffer from hunger and poverty.

Activity 1: Why are some people hungry?

A Sit with the children informally and pass around pictures of starving children in Africa. Ask them if they have ever stopped to think what it must be like to feel hungry all the time, not just at playtime when they can have a snack with their milk or at lunchtime when they are so hungry that they push to the front of the dinner queue or rush to open their lunchboxes to see what fillings are in their sandwiches today or what flavour crisps or yogurt they have. Ask them why they think some people are always hungry. They should tell you that it is because there is no food to eat. Explore with the children the reasons why.

B Show pupils two pictures and ask them to draw what they see for themselves: first, a beggar; second, a farmer standing in a parched field with withered crops all around him.

Look at the pictures they have drawn or painted and ask them what they think has caused the problem these two people have. Explain that the beggar has no money for food while the farmer cannot grow crops because of lack of rain and poor quality of soil.

To contrast lack of rain, paint a picture of a flood in front of the children and ask them to tell you what you are painting while you are doing it. Emphasise that floods can kill crops and people can go hungry for this reason. Consider the effect an earthquake has on people's lives and point out that this is another way in which crops die and people starve.

Now hold up two jars of water, one jar containing clean, fresh water and one dirty water. Ask the class which one they would drink. Tell them that in many parts of the world there is no clean water to drink and our bodies need clean water to work properly and keep us healthy. Explain that we all need food and water to survive. Without good, nourishing food we would all die.

C Tell the class about the Buddha at the time in his life when he was searching for the right way to live: he saw the poor and starving people in the streets in the city where he lived in India, was upset by what he saw and decided to starve himself. As you talk show the children one grain of rice in the palm of your hand and underline the fact that this was all that the Buddha ate every day for some time. Ask the children if they are surprised that the Buddha nearly died and if not, why not?

✓ On **Copymaster 26** (Would I feel hungry?), children can colour in the picture of the Buddha. They can tape a grain of rice on to the copymaster in the circle shown and underneath write how they would feel if they had only one grain of rice to eat per day.

Activity 2: What can we do to help provide food?

A Play the song 'Feed the World' to the class (Bob Geldolf, Live Aid Charity). Ask the children to listen carefully to the words and tell you afterwards what the song was about and what was being described (the famine). Write down some of the words as a list on the blackboard. Do these words make them feel sad? Why?

Ask them why they think the record was made. Tell them who Bob Geldolf is and say that he is just one person who is concerned about the starving people in Africa. Point to Africa on the world map. Explain that a lot of money can be made from selling records and this was one way Bob Geldolf helped the starving. Say that together you are going to look at different ways we can all help the hungry, prevent them from feeling sad and make them happy again.

B Make a list on the blackboard or a flipchart of the ways in which the children think they can help the hungry in the world. For example, they will recognise the names of some charities such as Oxfam and Save the Children. Ask them what they could do to help others through these charities rather than simply giving money which might take a long time to save up. Write down their ideas which might include giving jumble, wearing a red nose on Red Nose Day and raising money through sponsored events in school, knitting squares to make blankets to send warmth to the cold and starving, and so on.

They can make posters advertising these events and activities and place them around the school. Their posters can be given suitable titles – 'You can help' and 'Are you wearing your red nose today?' Provide plenty of materials so that posters can be made as eye-catching as possible.

C Tell the children about the work of Mother Teresa, explaining that she feels a great need to help the poor and starving in India, and through her faith in God she is able to carry on helping these people in great difficulty. The children can then write a short

F Ask the children to act out a play where a boy and girl come across a homeless, hungry person, living in a cardboard box under a railway station arch. Ask them to role-play what they would do after finding this person.

G Give out **Copymaster 27** (Helping hand) and ask children to match the person illustrated with the people they have helped who are poor and needy. They can then think of someone they could help, either in their own community or in another country, and link the two pictures at the foot of the sheet with a horizontal line.

description of Mother Teresa and her work, and draw a picture of her themselves.

Read **The bargain** (p. 35) to the children, tell them that the story takes place in the same country where Mother Teresa is hard at work and that the young boy, Nanak, who was later to become the founder of a faith in India called Sikhism, felt drawn to help the poor and needy in the story and get into trouble for it, rather than see the poor people he met starve to death.

H Ask the children to make a list of food they dislike and state what they don't like about it: they can work with a partner and discuss this while writing the information down. Bring all the children together and look at some of the lists. Discover with them which foods are disliked the most. Make a large bar graph called 'Foods we dislike' and study this with them. Ask them to imagine how much food they might turn away if all the food they disliked was offered to them?

Following on from this, ask the pupils to write a story about going to a friend's house where their friend's mother had prepared a meal containing food they did not like. Ask them to describe how they feel and what happens next. Do they try to eat the food or refuse it (politely or otherwise!)? Would it have been wrong to leave it all, if they did? Why? If they had managed to eat some of it, did they feel they had done the right thing, even though they did not like it? Why? Discuss with the class as a whole if it is right to leave unwanted food. Had they thought about the starving children in the world? Ask how many children would have written the story differently if they been thinking of children in other lands who cannot eat anything. Would it not have been better to say 'thank you' to their friend's mother anyway for the food they had been given?

D Tell the children that they might not have realised that there are people in our own country too who do have enough food to eat. Obtain posters of the Salvation Army feeding homeless people and display these in the classroom. Explain that members of the Salvation Army believe in Jesus Christ who helped the poor and fed the hungry: they feel they should carry on this work themselves today for people who need them and who are less fortunate than they are. Tell them this is why, even on cold, damp nights, they seek the homeless and hungry living on the streets and offer them hot soup and other nourishing foods to help them survive.

Play the children the song 'The Streets of London' and afterwards explain that in London, our capital city, there are many poor, hungry and homeless people wandering around, looking for food and shelter, and that the Salvation Army finds these people and feed them so that they will not starve. Ask the children how it would make them feel to be able to help these people like the Salvation Army do. Would they feel warm and happy inside? Write these words down on the blackboard next to the previous list of words which described the way they felt after hearing about the hungry in the song 'Feed the World'. Discuss the contrast in the words and suggest that they can make people in the world feel better and happier by offering help, however small. Revise here the topic song, **Food, food, food!**, and the happy/sad words noted.

I The children can write a prayer saying 'thank you' for food, to Mum for feeding them, to the dinner lady, to their friends' mothers, and finally to God for providing us with the food our families and friends give to us.

E Ask a member of the local Salvation Army to come into school to talk to the children about his or her work and faith.

J Read the stories **Breakfast by the lake** (p. 36) which tells of Jesus' love and care for his disciples by providing them with food when they really needed it, and **Lord Buddha's gift** (p. 36), telling of the time when the Buddha provides food for a little boy and his starving family because the boy believed in him and asked him for help. Draw pictures of the two stories in the form of 'before and after' scenes. More able children can pretend to be a character from one of the stories and write a few lines about how they felt at the time of the miracle.

GREED

Purpose

To explore the effects of greed, feeling too full and looking at how we can stay healthy.

Activity 1: Feeling too full

Note While doing this work it is important to be sensitive to children in the class who may be overweight. Emphasise that being overweight may be the result of medical conditions or characteristics inherited from our families (see Big Me and Little Me, p. 3). However, stress that, whatever our circumstances, we can all help ourselves by regulating the type and amount of food we eat.

A Sit the children in front of the blackboard or a flipchart. Tell them you are going to draw two people, one who is called Mr Fat and the other who is called Mrs Fit. Sketch these people in front of the children and ask them to point out the differences between the two figures. What are Mr Fat and Mrs Fit wearing? Do their clothes fit their figures well? Ask them how much food they think Mr Fat eats and how much Mrs Fit eats. How do they know?

Afterwards, ask them if they have ever felt too full, and if they can give you some words to describe what this feels like such as 'fat', 'blown up', 'round', 'heavy', etc. Ask them if they feel full of energy when they have eaten too much. Do they want to leap about or curl up in a chair and go to sleep? Talk about Mrs Fit. What effect did eating just enough healthy food have on her? Did she enjoy living more than Mr Fat? Why?

B Look at a picture of an overweight person with the children. Explain that this person looks at least four stones overweight in the picture. Produce four one-stone bags of potatoes and give the bags to individual children to carry. Point out that the children find the weight of each bag on its own is very heavy. Get them to imagine the weight of all the bags put together being

carried around by a person who is at least that much overweight. What would the person feel like? Explain it would be doing the person harm to have so much extra weight to carry about. Tell them that some fat is necessary because it helps to keep us warm when it is cold and can give us valuable energy when we have not eaten for a while. Emphasise that too much fat can be harmful to our heart which has to work harder than it should do in order for us to move around. Show children the picture of the overweight person again. Then show them a picture of a fit, healthy person. Remind the children of the sort of foods they think the overweight and the healthy person might be eating.

Copymaster 28 (Mr Fat and Mrs Fit) gives pupils the opportunity to colour pictures of Mr Fat and Mrs Fit. Underneath they should write down the type of food that both might eat.

C Explain to the children that foods we eat contain different properties and nutrients which carry out different tasks in the body: some help us to grow strong, others give us energy, and others keep us fit and healthy. Divide the class into three large groups representing each category: 'Food for growing', 'Energy foods' and 'Vitamin-rich foods'. Ask each group to collect simple 'food facts' from information prepared earlier by you – a ring binder comprising sheets which can be detached and passed around is ideal (see p. 33).

Still working in their groups, invite pupils to make a food wall frieze under the three main sections. They can draw or paint pictures, cut out photographs from magazines and food leaflets, and collect wrappers or packaging and stick them on to the display to give a two-dimensional effect.

Now attempt **Copymaster 29** (Food groups). Pupils should colour in the pictures of foods, then decide to which of the three groups each item belongs by putting

Food binders

the letter 'G' (food for growing), 'E' (energy foods) or 'V' (vitamin-rich foods) in the box provided. Display completed copymasters alongside the wall frieze.

D Ask the children why we should exercise as well as eat the right foods in order to stay healthy. Show them a picture of an athlete and ask them to describe their appearance. Ask the children what this athlete has to be careful about in order to stay fit and healthy and be a good sportsperson. Remind pupils that it is not recommended to exercise straight after eating and ask them if they know why.

E Use **Copymaster 30** (My food for the day) for the children to plan a daily menu. Advise them to decide upon foods which will provide energy, vitamins and will make them grow strong. Discuss with them the possibility of replacing snacks such as chocolate biscuits and crisps with healthier options like fruit and nuts. The sheet can be copied seven times to cover each day of the week. When children have completed the work, sheets can be stapled together and taken home to show to parents.

F Make a poster called 'Our ideal healthy school lunch', which can be worked out collectively by the class after they have finished their individual menus. They can cut out pictures of food from magazines and decorate their menu with these pictures. Suggest that the poster is displayed in the school dining hall.

Area of study 4

CELEBRATION FOOD ▶

Purpose
To show the importance of food as part of celebration.

Activity 1: Looking at celebration food

A Sit the children informally and ask them if anybody has had a birthday recently. Ask the child concerned if he or she had a special birthday tea or meal and what he or she ate to celebrate. Remind pupils of their class party (see **Birth celebrations**, p. 19) and note the foods they liked best.

B Consider together the different shapes and designs used for birthday cakes – train-shaped, heart-shaped, balloon-shaped, round, square, etc. – and tell children that they are to design their ideal cake, deciding not only how it will look but also what it contains and how many candles should be on top. Encourage them to plan out their ideas on rough paper, before drawing, decorating and writing about the cake on a large piece of paper.

C Show the children a picture of the Nativity scene around the manger. Ask them what this picture is all about and remind them that at Christmas, Christians or followers of Christ, celebrate his coming to earth. Discuss what food is served up at Christmas dinner and then ask the class why a big meal is eaten at this festival.

The children can draw a bird's-eye view of the main course for Christmas dinner and label the foods on the plate. Mention to them that Christians say a special grace at this time thanking God for their food and for sending his son, Jesus Christ, to earth.

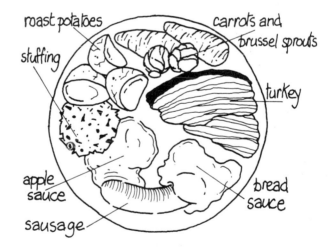

D Now show the children a chocolate egg. Ask them what time of year we eat chocolate eggs and why? Show them a picture of a chicken and an egg. Say the chicken broke out of the eggshell when it was time to be born and in the same way, Christians believe that Jesus broke free from the tomb in which he was buried after his death to rise up and live again among those who believed in him.

The children can make their own Easter eggs by decorating eggshells with colourful patterns remembering that the custom of eating eggs at Easter is practised by followers around the world.

E Read the account of the Last Supper (Matthew 26:20–9). Jesus shares a meal of bread and wine with his friends – the disciples or followers. Ask the children if they know why the food is so important in this story. Explain to them that ever since his death, Christians have remembered Jesus by eating bread (or wafers) and wine at a special service in church. Tell the children to write down the words in the biblical account which refer to the bread and wine and why they are specially related to Jesus. Incorporate these words into simple drawings showing pictures of the foods framed by an illustrative border of wheat and grapes.

Ask the children to role-play the scene of the Last Supper and show Jesus breaking the bread and passing a cup full of wine around his disciples. Ask a child to narrate the story at this scene while it is being acted.

F Show the children a picture of the countryside at harvest time with the plough and the fields full of bales of hay. Then show the children the inside of a church at harvest, where the food has been gathered in and put on display for people to see at their Harvest Thanksgiving Service. Examine what is in the display, namely flowers, fruit, vegetables, and tins of produce, and explain that Christians go to church to thank God for their food at this time. Ask them to write a special Harvest Prayer thanking God for the food he has given which they should never take for granted. The children can paint pictures of harvest time – either a countryside scene or a Harvest Festival display in church.

Activity 2: Celebration food in other world faiths
A Show the children a tree branch and ask them to identify it. Explain that followers of the Jewish faith called Jews also celebrate Harvest Festival as 'Succoth' or the Feast of Tabernacles. Write these names on the blackboard and tell the class that it is at this festival of celebration that Jews remember their people's escape from Egypt and their wandering in the wilderness for 40 years. Branches of trees like the one they see in front of them were used as decorations during the ceremonies and special food (cheese-filled pancakes and dairy products) and drink is taken inside a hut, specially built inside Jewish homes for the festival.

Ask the children to draw a picture of Jewish children carrying tree branches towards the hut for the celebration.

B Show the children samples of the following foods on a large plate: *matzah* bread, bitter herbs, lettuce. A cup containing wine should be placed by the side of the plate. Explain that the food they see is very special food given to celebrate the Jewish Passover Festival. Explain what the Passover Festival is and how on the first night of the Festival a very special meal is served in every Jewish household: this is called the Seder meal. Write this word down on card and place it immediately below the plate, centrally. Write the words 'matzah', 'bitter herbs', 'lettuce' and 'wine' on separate cards and place them by the food on the plate for the children to see. Tell the children what the foods represent: the bitter herbs show the Jews' suffering in Egypt; the lettuce welcomes spring and the wine represents freedom.

C Obtain a recipe from a Jewish cook book and make *matzah* bread with the children. Ask them to sample it and describe its taste. Then do the same with the other foods. The children can make a special recipe card, 'The Seder meal'.

D Talk to the children about the followers of the faith of Allah known as Muslims and explain that they celebrate a festival called 'Eid-ul-Fitr' which means 'a little festival'. Here food is particularly important as the Muslims have been fasting or eating no food between when the sun rises and sets each day for a month. Tell the children that part of their celebration is to take special sweets to members of their community less fortunate than they are. Show the children a small sample of these Eid sweets arranged on a plate. The children can then make models of these sweets, using Plaster of Paris or clay; after they have set or been fired they can be painted in bright colours. They can then draw a picture of the sweets and write down the recipe on a special card.

E Ask the children to close their eyes and think of springtime. After a few moments, they can open their eyes and tell you what they associate with this time of year. Maybe they have thought about buds on trees and the days becoming longer and brighter. Explain to them that followers of the Hindu and Sikh faiths think that spring is very special and celebrate this new season by, among other activities, giving and sharing food.

Tell the children that Hindu and Sikh children particularly enjoy this celebration because they feel very happy – dancing, playing games, squirting coloured water at each other and then in the afternoon sharing a big celebration meal. Say that examples of food eaten at the meal might be *puri*, a type of bread fried in butter; *matar panir*, a vegetable curry with peas, curd cheese, and rice. If possible, show the children pictures of the type of foods eaten at this celebration. They can draw these dishes on cards to add to their resource bank of celebration food.

F Finally, throughout this activity the children will have been collecting paintings, pictures and recipes of the different types of food eaten at festival celebrations. They can now form these into a colourful book which should be laid out so that an illustration, child's drawing or recipe appears on the left-hand page and on the opposite page there is any necessary written material. They can label the pictures and write a little about each food on the right-hand page. The booklet can be called 'Celebration food' and include a contents page which should contain the name of the celebration food, the name of the festival with which it is connected in parentheses after it, and the page number.

TOPIC STORIES

The bargain

When Guru Nanak, the founder of the Sikh faith, was a boy, he lived in the village of Talwandi in Northern India. Nanak was always kind to poorer children in the village and always shared his sweets with them. Sometimes he took them all to his home and his mother made cakes and more sweets for his friends.

One day Nanak's father said, 'Nanak, you'll never be a good business man if you keep giving everything away. Now listen to me carefully. I am going to give you twenty rupees. I want you to go into the other villages or the town and buy something useful for our farm. You must bargain carefully and buy something good.'

'Oh, yes, father,' said Nanak. 'I will buy something useful.'

'Just to make sure you don't give the money away I will send Bala, our servant with you and he will look after the twenty rupees,' said Nanak's father.

Bala was only a few years older than Nanak and the two boys set off happily, looking forward to a day out. They chatted and sang as they walked from Talwandi through the nearby villages.

'Let's go on until we find a big village or a town,' Nanak said. 'We don't have to be back until nightfall so we can have some fun.'

The boys climbed trees and had a wonderful time. They ate the food Nanak's mother had prepared for them and at midday they reached the outskirts of a large town.

'There is sure to be a market here and you'll be able to make your bargain,' said Bala. 'Buy something for the farm as your father told you.'

Nanak agreed but as the boys entered the town some poor holy men called to them.

'The people of the town won't give us any food and we are starving,' they told them.

Nanak looked at the holy men. They looked thin and ill and their clothes were in rags.

'Nanak, come on. Take no notice –' Bala tugged at Nanak's arm.

'They look so thin and ill,' said Nanak. 'Give them the twenty rupees, Bala.'

'No, Nanak. I can't. Your father will be angry,' argued Bala. 'Your father says you must make a bargain with the money.'

'Bala, please do as I ask. These men are starving,' answered Nanak. 'Give them the money.'

Bala shook his head and began to walk away. Nanak ran after him.

'Bala, please. My father won't be angry with you. I'll tell him I did this myself. He'll know that anyway.'

Bala handed him the twenty rupees but he wasn't happy about it and even when the holy men thanked him and Nanak and said the boys had saved their lives, Bala was still unhappy.

'Well, we've no money now. Let's just have some fun,' said Nanak and because the two boys were such good friends they were soon running about the town enjoying themselves.

It was only much later when Nanak and Bala were almost back in their village that Nanak became frightened.

'I'm going to stay in our tree house tonight,' he told Bala. 'I'll speak to my father in the morning.'

'But he'll be waiting for us. He'll want to know about your bargain,' said Bala.

'You stay here with me then,' replied Nanak.

'I'll go straight to my room,' said Bala and he hurried to the back of the farmhouse where the family servants slept.

Nanak's father waited until darkness fell and went to the servants' rooms to find Bala.

'Where is Nanak?' he asked sternly.

'Oh – he's – staying out tonight – on the farm,' stammered Bala.

'Oh? Is he trying out the new bargain he got?' asked Nanak's father.

'Oh – he might be.' Bala did not want to give his friend away.

'What do you mean?' cried Nanak's father. 'Did he get a bargain or didn't he? Answer me, Bala.'

Bala hung his head. Nanak's father turned away and went straight to the tree house where he knew Nanak would be hiding. He shook the tree hard.

'Nanak, come down. I know you are up there,' he shouted.

Nanak came down slowly. His father was really angry.

'Where is this bargain I sent you to buy?' he asked sharply.

'I – I gave the money to some holy men,' admitted Nanak.

If Nanak's mother and sisters had not come running from the house at that moment, Nanak's father would have slapped him hard.

'Father, you know Nanak can't bear to see anyone hungry and starving,' said Nanaki, Nanak's sister, who ran in front of her brother to protect him. 'You'll never change him.'

When Nanak was born, a priest had told the child's father that Nanak would one day be a great holy man. As he walked back to the house, still angry with his son, Nanak's father wondered what was to become of the boy. He did not understand that Nanaki, his daughter was right. Nanak could not bear to see people hungry and would always give whatever he had to help them – though in future it would be his own money he would give to the poor, and not his father's.

Nanak was loved by the poor people wherever he went and he always did his best to help them.

Breakfast by the lake

The fishermen had been out on Lake Galilee all night but hadn't caught any fish and they were cross and tired.

'There can't be any fish left in this lake. They've all gone somewhere else,' grumbled Peter, the tall fisherman, as he and his brother Andrew dragged the empty trawl net back into the boat. 'Whose idea was it to spend the night on the lake anyway?'

'We all agreed to try,' said John quietly. 'I'm sure we'll find some fish soon.'

'I don't think we will,' answered Peter. 'And look, the sky is becoming lighter. It's nearly dawn. I think we should make our way back to the shore.'

The others agreed sadly. It had been a wasted night for all of them.

As they turned the boat towards the shore, they saw a tall figure standing at the water's edge.

'Someone is up early,' said James, John's brother. 'I wonder who it is and what he's doing there?'

'Perhaps he's a fisherman too, and couldn't find any fish,' replied John.

As they steered the boat in the direction of the stranger, Peter shouted and waved to the man who waved back.

'You are fishing on the wrong side of the lake,' called the man. 'Take the boat out again, over there.' He pointed to the opposite side of the water. 'You'll find plenty of fish there.'

'Come on, it's worth a try,' Andrew said.

'Oh – I don't know –' began Peter but James and John agreed with Andrew.

'We've been out all night. What difference does another hour make?' James asked and the boat sailed away with Peter and Andrew standing ready to cast out the net.

A few minutes later the net was so full of fish that it took all four fishermen to drag it into the boat.

'I've never seen anything like this,' cried Peter. 'That man knew what he was talking about.'

'We must go back and thank him,' said John. 'That's if he's still there.'

A few yards from the shore they saw the stranger.

'Come and have your breakfast,' he called to them. He was bending over a fire and the smell of cooked fish reminded the fishermen how hungry they were.

Peter was staring at the stranger and suddenly he leapt out of the boat, nearly capsizing it.

'Peter, what do you think you are doing?' shouted James as he and the others tried to steady the boat.

'It's the Lord. It's Jesus!' shouted Peter as he waded through the water to the shore.

Jesus was waiting as the others scrambled after Peter to join him.

'Is it really you, Lord?' asked John, shyly.

It seemed so long since Jesus had left them to go to heaven. The disciples had done as Jesus had asked and gone home to Galilee. Now, here he was, caring for them as usual, finding food for them when they needed it. The disciples knew Jesus would not be able to stay with them for long but that breakfast on the sea shore was one of the happiest they had known.

Lord Buddha's gift

Seeva was the youngest child of a poor farmer and his wife who lived in the Indian state of Nepal. The farmer had one field in which he grew grain which he sold once a year in a nearby market. If his crops had done well he would make enough money to feed and clothe his family until the next harvest but if not, the farmer and his family would have to go hungry.

One year the grain did not grow well at all. The farmer went into his field every day to try to save his crop but he could see that there would be a poor harvest and he would not earn enough money to keep the family fed and clothed until the following year.

Seeva always followed his father into the field and he knew how worried his parents were.

'Why don't you take some of the grain to the Temple and ask Lord Buddha for his help?' the little boy asked.

'Seeva, we can't spare any grain at all,' answered his father.

'Not even a few handfuls for Lord Buddha?' asked Seeva, sadly.

'No, Seeva, not even a few handfuls.'

The farmer turned away and Seeva stared after him. Surely his father knew that Lord Buddha would help if he was asked to do so.

Seeva waited until his father had gone into the house and then he carefully gathered a few handfuls of grain and hurried out of the field. He made his way through their small village until he came to an old temple. He took off his shoes and entered quietly, making his way to the large golden statue of the Buddha at the front of the temple. He placed the handful of grain before the statue and thought to himself, 'No one has brought the Lord Buddha any food for a long time. There isn't any here.'

Most of the villagers were having trouble with their crops, too. It had been a hot, dry summer and the crops were thirsty. No one but Seeva had thought of taking any of their precious grain to Lord Buddha.

'Please, Lord Buddha, help our crops to grow,' prayed Seeva before the statue. 'I know you don't want us to starve.'

When Seeva arrived home, his mother and father were cross with him and his brothers and sisters laughed at him and told him he was stupid.

'I thought I told you we hadn't any grain to spare for Lord Buddha,' Seeva's father said, angrily. 'You shouldn't have disobeyed me, Seeva.'

It was even worse a few days later because the birds ate most of the grain before the farmer could gather it in.

'A lot of good it did to go to Lord Buddha, didn't it?' teased Seeva's brothers. 'We've lost all our grain now.'

Seeva said nothing. He was disappointed in Lord Buddha. He had asked for his help and everything was much worse.

'I'm going to tell Lord Buddha he's made everything worse,' thought Seeva. 'Perhaps he'll help us this time.'

'Seeva has gone to the temple again,' one of the little boy's sisters told her father.

'Oh, well, let him go. It won't make much difference now,' answered the farmer.

Seeva crept into the temple and made his way to the statue of Lord Buddha. He looked for his handful of grain but it was nowhere to be seen.

'Someone's taken it,' he thought. 'I wonder who could have taken it and left Lord Buddha with none at all.'

Seeva turned to make his way out of the temple and then he was staring at the corner of the temple in amazement and delight. A large pile of grain was gleaming in the half light. Seeva ran all the way home and into the house.

'Quick! Bring sacks!' he shouted. 'Lord Buddha has blessed the grain I took him and given us much more.'

His father and brothers took some sacks and followed Seeva back to the temple. They filled all the sacks and had to go back for more.

'You see, Lord Buddha did answer my prayers,' cried Seeva when, at last, all the sacks of grain were safely stored in the house.

'Yes, Seeva, you are right,' answered his father. 'You have shown us exactly what we should have done. You had faith in Lord Buddha and he has rewarded all of us. Now we will certainly have enough to see us through until next year.'

As the farmer and his older sons talked about going to market, Seeva slipped back to the temple to thank Lord Buddha for answering his prayer.

Worship

Places of worship (Christian)

- Looking at a Christian building
- Symbols
- In church

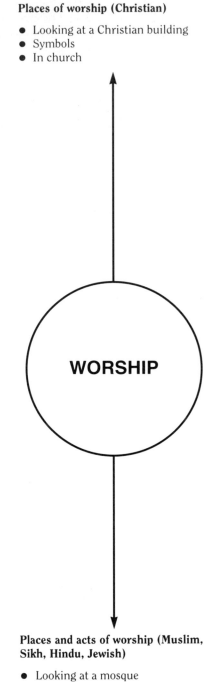

WORSHIP

Places and acts of worship (Muslim, Sikh, Hindu, Jewish)

- Looking at a mosque
- Looking at a gurdwara
- Looking at a Hindu home shrine
- Focus on a Jewish synagogue and the importance of prayer

LEARNING OBJECTIVES

- To be aware that believing in God is important for many people and that worship takes place at home and in special places.
- To be familiar with rules and customs which influence and affect people's lives.
- To recognise special places of worship and the practice of religion in the family.
- To be able to give some examples of religious teachings which influence our daily lives.
- To associate the celebration of special family events and seasonal religious festivals with places of worship.
- To be able to identify people connected with worship (i.e. vicar, priest, imam, rabbi) and to be aware of contrasting forms of worship.

STARTING POINTS

- Show the children contrasting pictures from books or magazines of worship taking place in the home and at a special place of worship. This might be a Hindu family in front of a home shrine or a congregation in a church. Ask the children if they know what is happening in the pictures and point out to them the contrast in the different ways people need to worship.

- Discuss as many different places of worship as possible to be found in the community: for example, a church, a mosque, a synagogue, a prayer hall, and so on. What are the differences between the buildings? Why does a church have a spire or tower? Why does a mosque have a tower? What does the synagogue look like?

- Present the children with a collection of colourful books containing pictures of people they would find in the buildings they have discussed. Ask them who belongs in each building. They can then draw these people, looking carefully at what they are wearing, and choosing their colours with care.

- Have ready a hand torch and switch it on. Ask the children to describe the light from the torch. Then show

them a candle. Ask them to describe the appearance of the candle. If possible in school, light the candle. If not, ask the children to imagine the candle lit up. What is the flame of a candle like? How is it different from the light of the torch? Point out that a candle gives off a living flame and that it is used in worship by millions of people all over the world. Explain that you will all be looking at other objects of worship that are important to many different people.

- Ask the children to draw themselves in their best clothes. Look at these pictures informally with the children and talk about the clothes. Ask the children when they would wear these clothes. Say that many people wear special clothes when they go to worship. Ask them why they think this happens.

- Ask the children to imagine walking into a place of worship. What colours would they see? Do a lot of colours make a place more beautiful? What can they smell? What can they hear? Jot down their answers on the blackboard or on a flipchart.

- Teach the topic song, **Worship you.**

PLACES OF WORSHIP

Purpose

To familiarise the children with the external and internal aspects of a traditional Christian church and the activities carried out by Christian worshippers.

Activity 1: Introduction to worship

Sit with the children around a central table which is covered with a clean white tablecloth concealing a number of objects. Ask the children to sit quietly for a few moments when the cloth is removed and to look carefully at the article on the table which they like best. Objects might be a silver or gold ball, a crystal paperweight through which the light shines, a particularly attractive flower arrangement or a mirror

against which shells, coloured stones or glass animals are reflected.

Talk with the children informally about events taking place in school collective worship and any occasions when they have attended places of worship, writing the word 'worship' on the blackboard for the children to practise using.

Activity 2: Symbols

A Use **Copymaster 31** (The Christian symbol) to examine together the most universal symbol of the Christian faith and where the cross might be found (inside churches, chapels and cathedrals, in Christian books, worn around the neck as jewellery, etc.). The

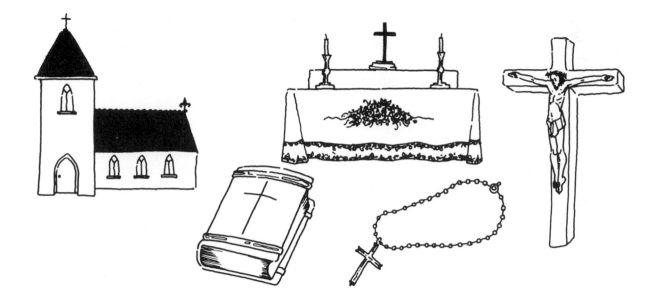

children select the correct words to match the pictures and fill in the blanks to remind themselves where they might come across the symbol.

Find out whether the children are aware of the importance of the cross and why it is the main symbol of the Christian faith.

B Read the story **The little donkey** (p. 46) to the children. Discuss this in relation to Palm Sunday, showing the children palm crosses. Tell them about significant events during the last week before the Crucifixion (though not details of the event itself).

C Make a collage or wall frieze of the Palm Sunday story. Create huge palm leaves or banners on which pupils' work can be displayed.

Activity 3: In church

A Sit with the children and show them photographs of people at worship, beginning with pictures of special assembly service or church services in which pupils from their own school are participating. Look at the ways in which children are praying or talking to God or just being still and quiet. Consider any prayers which are often said in school and talk about their meaning together, writing significant words or phrases on the board.

B Give the children paper and crayons and ask them to make up prayers of their own: they could be for members of the family, a child in the class who is ill, a classroom pet, or simply to say 'thank you' to God for his wonderful gifts (cross-reference **Food**, p. 34). Let the children make their prayers as attractive as possible, writing their names at the top. Hang them around the room or on a special 'prayer tree' made of cardboard in a corner of the classroom.

C Show the children further photographs of people at worship, identifying the vicar, priest or minister, the congregation and different parts of the interior of the church.

D Arrange a special service (i.e. Christmas, Harvest, Easter) with the vicar of a traditional Anglican church. Invite the vicar to come to the school and plan the event with the children. Pupils can devise their own prayers and select hymns according to the season. Ask the vicar to explain to the children exactly what he will be doing and the vestments he will be wearing on this occasion.

Now attempt **Copymaster 32** (Vicar's vestments). Study the pictures of the priest's vestments with the children. They can label the different parts of dress and

underneath colour in the boxes in the colour worn to indicate different seasons of the Christian year.

E Take the class to the church for a rehearsal for their special service, stressing the need to enter quietly and reverently.

✔ Before the rehearsal, give each child **Copymaster 33** (Church jigsaw). They can ask the vicar if he will assist in pointing out the structure of the church in addition to the items depicted on the copymaster. When they return to school children can work in pairs and cut out the 'jigsaw' pieces from one copymaster while the sheet belonging to the second partner is kept intact. Now the pieces should be jumbled and rearranged in the correct order by both partners using the uncut sheet as a guide.

F Let the children advertise their special service by making invitations and posters. Invite the rest of the school, parents, governors and friends to the service so

that, as well as participating in an important church event, children can see for themselves how the members of the congregation participate.

PLACES AND ACTS OF WORSHIP (MUSLIM, SIKH, HINDU, JEWISH)

Area of study 2

C34 –40

Purpose
To introduce children to examples of places of worship other than Christian.

Activity 1: Looking at a mosque
A Show the children slides of the Ka'aba in Mecca. Remind them of the story of the Prophet Muhammad's birth (see p. 24), that he would walk every day to the Ka'aba to worship there in the mosque, the Muslim place of worship which today is the most holy place of worship for all Muslims. Sit with the children informally and, using a large picture of Mecca and the Ka'aba, tell the story of the Prophet Muhammad and the spread of Islam. Key words can be accompanied by flashcards: 'Muslim', 'mosque', 'Allah', 'idols', etc. Point out the direction the worshippers face, explaining that they always face the direction in which Mecca is when they worship.

B Arrange a visit to a local mosque or, alternatively, invite a local imam to speak to the children in school. If visiting the mosque, children will have first-hand experience of removing shoes and seeing the Ablutions Room as well as Muslims at prayer and the necessity for quietness in worship. Tell the children about or ask the imam to point out the room where Muslim boys and girls learn Arabic for the purpose of reading and understanding the Qu'ran, the Muslim holy book. If possible, visit the mosque shop in an Islamic Centre.

C On returning to school, divide the class into several groups containing eight children. Provide each group with one copy of **Copymaster 34** (Building a mosque) and an A3-sized plan of a mosque, simplfied as below.

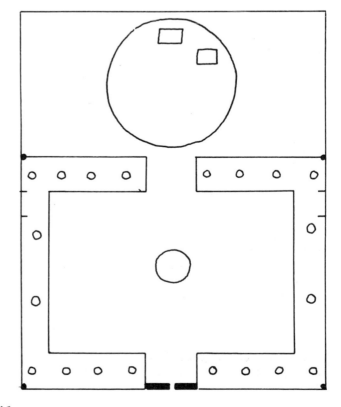

Each child in the group takes one picture to colour when it has been cut out, then with your help pins it on to the plan in the correct place.

D Erect a class model of a mosque from thick cardboard. Include features such as the dome and minaret. The walls can be decorated with intricate Islamic patterns.

E Read the story **The Prophet Muhammad** (p. 47) which tells how Muhammad once transformed the way Muslims worshipped in the mosque.

Activity 2: Looking at a gurdwara

A Show the children slides of the Golden Temple at Amritsar which stands upon land given to the Sikhs by the Muslim Emperor Akbar. Remind them of Guru Nanak and the stories connected with him. Arrange with the gurdwara committee at a local Sikh temple for children to attend a naming ceremony and invite the family to a special tea in school beforehand so that the children will know the child does not yet have an official name and will be waiting for his or her name to be given at the ceremony.

B Show children **Copymaster 35** (Gurdwara I-spy), to familiarise them with the building they will see and the people they will meet. Ask them to notice details and events such as removing shoes, covering heads and washing hands, where men and women sit, the position of Guru Granth Sahib and the granthi or reader. When they return to the classroom, pupils can tick the important objects or people they have seen at the gurdwara. Should such a visit not be possible, Programme Four, 'Symbols of Faith and Justice', of *Coming Together* will be a viable alternative, though this is for the temple layout and services only.

C A similar visit to a gurdwara might be made for a small part of the marriage ceremony, though a video can easily be obtained by arrangement with local gurdwaras or through the Sikh representative at the Standing Advisory Council on Religious Education (SACRE). Children may like to draw pictures of the red and gold *sari* or *shalwar* and *kameez* of the bride and the garlanded bridegroom.

D Sit with the children informally and tell them that as well as going to a gurdwara, Sikhs set up special places in their home where they can pray and worship. Show photographs of Sikh home shrines, explaining that a copy of Guru Granth Sahib must be in every shrine.

Activity 3: Hindu gods, the caste system, and worship in a Hindu temple

A Invite someone the children know well such as a dinner lady, lollipop man/lady or the school caretaker to sit in front of the class. Give the children paper and pencil and ask them to draw the visitor. Compare the pictures afterwards, considering how many different ideas of someone there can be. Look at the various attitudes the children have shown. Discuss whether it might be possible to put all the pictures together to form one person or whether they can agree that someone has many sides to their personality.

B Show the children large posters of Hindu gods: Vishnu, Shiva, Krishna, Lakshmi and Ganesh. Explain that all these and many more are different ideas of the same God who, according to Hindu belief, has many forms. Let the children comment on each picture, working out what the god is wearing and how he or she is sitting.

Hold up the picture of Vishnu again. Explain that many Hindus believe that Vishnu is the true god. He sits on a large snake which has many heads and Vishnu has four arms to show that he rules the whole world. He holds a conch shell which Indian warriors blew as a sign that battle was about to commence. Tell them that Vishnu's skin is blue and his clothes are yellow and he comes to save the world when it is in danger.

Show the children Shiva. Explain that Shiva is thought to have danced the world into creation and he carries a small drum as he also created sound. Tell them that Shiva is said to be able to destroy the world and he also holds fire. 'Shiva' means 'kindly' and his vehicle is Nandi, the bull.

Krishna   Lakshmi   Shiva   Vishnu   Ganesh

C Read the information about **Ganesh** to the children (p. 47). Now show them the picture of Krishna again. Explain that he is also a favourite god and that there are many temples named for him. Krishna is thought to be the Lord of all by many Hindus and is usually seen playing his flute. He gave the *Bhavagad Gita*, the Hindu holy book, to Hindus. Explain that as a boy, in the kingdom of Nandi the cowherd, he danced with the milkmaids in the moonlight. He married Radha, his favourite milkmaid and she is usually seen with him in Hindu temples.

Give the children drawings of the gods and ask them to put the correct names by the pictures and say underneath which god they like best and why. Pupils can make stand-up figures of the gods, supported at the back like a photograph or picture backing.

D Sit with the children around a large map of ancient India showing the Indus valley. Write the names 'Aryans' and 'Dravidians' on large pieces of card and pass these around the class, letting the children practise saying the names out aloud to each other. Now ask them to close their eyes and imagine they are stepping into a large shining time machine. They will be travelling back 5 000 years and when the machine stops they will be stepping out on green grass and at the home of Seeva, a dark-haired, dark-skinned boy of their own age who helps his father and brothers to run a big farm. In the fields rice and vegetables are grown and once every week Seeva and his brothers take the rice and fresh vegetables by boat to Harappa, the large city further inland.

When they open their eyes, write 'Seeva the Dravidian' on the board, then read **Seeva's story** (p. 47). Afterwards, consider together how Seeva must have felt to have everything changed so drastically.

E Take the children to the school library and help them to find any pictures of old India and its early inhabitants. Then use **Copymaster 36** (Hindu origins and castes) and ask pupils to fill in the River Indus and the Indus Valley on the map of India and then complete the blanks underneath the pictures representing people from the four castes in existence in India.

Divide a large sheet of paper into two columns

headed 'Aryans' and 'Dravidians'. In each column the children should write the kind of jobs each sect might be expected to do, such as taking prayers, fighting, selling grain, spices and clothes, working in the fields or fetching and carrying for others.

F Show the children a photograph of Hindus at worship in a temple. Write the name Mandir on the blackboard so that children can practise saying it and beside it write its meaning: 'place of worship'. Identify in the photograph the actions of the worshippers and explain that Hindu temples are meant to face the rising sun and in India they often stand within a walled enclosure.

G Contact the Education Department of the nearest Hindu temple and invite a priest or someone able to lead worship to visit the class. Arrange artefacts used in the temple on a table for the children to see clearly – a statue or statues of gods in the temple to which the visitor belongs, a conch shell, incense sticks, three small bells and, if possible, a set of Indian drums. Ask the visitor to explain the importance of each artefact to temple worship.

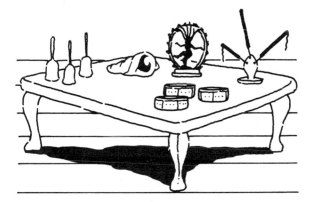

H Read to the children the story of **Ram the priest** (p. 48) and invite the visitor to explain any differences with British temple worship.

I Arrange with the visitor to take the children to a Hindu temple. Provide each pupil with **Copymaster 37** (Hindu temple I-spy), so that they can identify the objects on the sheet while walking around the building and place a tick in the boxes to show that they have seen them.

J Read the children the following description of prayer at a Hindu home shrine:

Sushila Patel gets up early in the morning, has a bath and puts on clean clothes. She prepares food for her family but first she takes a special bowl and offers food to Krishna, the god worshipped by the family. Sushila lights a small *divas* lamp and an incense stick and says her morning prayers.

That evening the whole family gather in front of the home shrine which is in a corner of their living room. Everyone is clean and tidy, and no one is wearing shoes. Sushila's husband, Bikhu, leads the family prayers this time.

43

Ask the children where they would find the Patel family's home shrine.

K Read the children the following prayer which might end the service at a home shrine:

> May there be peace in Heaven.
> May there be peace in the skies.
> May there be peace on earth.
> May there be peace in the waters.
> May there be peace in the plants.
> May there be peace in the trees.
> May we find peace in the supreme Lord.
> May we all be in peace.
> May that peace be mine.
> Peace. Peace. Peace.

L Look with the children at a modern map of India showing Calcutta where Ram the priest can be found in his temple. Play a recording of Hindu conch shells and explain that these might have been used 4 000 years ago for the calling of the warriors into battle.

Tell the children that in Calcutta nowadays as the sun goes down, conch shells are heard calling Hindus to prayer. Explain that when the worshipper enters the temple, he or she will ring a bell over the entrance to let God know how he or she has arrived for worship. Tell the children that in British temples the bells announce worship in the same way.

Activity 4: The Jewish synagogue and the importance of prayer

A Use the daily storytime session to tell the story of Moses. Remind the children of the Israelite baby who was adopted by the Egyptian princess and whom everyone thought was a prince of Egypt and read the account of Moses from this time in **The last plague** (p. 48).

B Make a list of the kind of articles each family would need to pack for such a departure and read the story of **The escape** (p. 49). The video of the film *The Ten Commandments* is widely available and gives a vivid and colourful presentation of how the Exodus might have been. Explain that the Israelites Moses led into the

desert (or wilderness) became the first Jewish nation. Therefore, Moses founded the religion known as Judaism.

C As a class, create a timeline to reinforce the order of events of the Exodus, including the 'Passing Over' of Israelites' homes by Death, the messenger rushing through the streets, the last meal (lamb, unleavened bread) and the eventual departure and Red Sea crossing. Mark each event clearly along the timeline by drawing diagrams and annotated labels.

D Show the children large pictures of Moses and the Israelites in the desert. Explain that the Israelites had been slaves for so long that they did not know how to behave when they choose for themselves how to act towards each other: they fought and killed each other and many of them forgot God entirely.

A simple version of the Ten Commandments is given on **Copymaster 38** (The Ten Commandments). The children can read the Commandments out loud and then colour in the letters, using a different colour for each Commandment. They can then cut out the Commandments and stick them on to coloured cards.

E Arrange a visit to a local Orthodox synagogue. First talk with the children about everything they will see there and make caps or *yarmulkas* for the boys to wear.

Invite the rabbi into school first to discuss with the children the plan of the synagogue and the layout of the building.

When the children visit the synagogue, give them **Copymaster 39** (Plan of a synagogue) and ask them to complete it as they do their tour. When they enter the building they should stand still and feel its atmosphere of peace and stillness. It will be explained to the children that the Holy Scriptures play a very important part in Jewish worship and that these can be found in the Old Testament of the Bible and are divided into three sections: the Torah, the Prophets and the Writings. Show the children the language of Hebrew in which Jewish Scriptures are written, noting that this is written from right to left. Tell the children that the Torah or five books of Moses tell of the origins of the Jewish people from Creation through Abraham to Moses: they show Jews how to live within the laws of God and are called Genesis, Exodus, Numbers, Leviticus and Deuteronomy. Explain that books of the Scriptures are written in scrolls which are placed round wooden rollers. Each roller is known as the 'Tree of Life'. Tell the children that these scrolls are written by a specially trained religious scribe who uses a feather pen and *kosher* vegetable ink which lasts for a long time.

The rabbi will be able to explain to the children why the scrolls are contained by a special covering and why the Torah has a breastplate and a silver pointer and is decorated with bells (the High Priest of ancient Judaism wore bells and a breastplate as part of his dress). It is a high honour to be given the special task of taking the scrolls from the ark. First, the curtain will be pulled back gently and carefully and the scrolls will be shown to the congregation who will be standing and will say, 'Blessed is he who in his holiness gave the Law to his people Israel'. When the scroll is lifted gently from the ark and given to the reader, he and the congregation will say, 'Hear, O Israel, the Lord our God. The Lord is One. One is our God. Holy is His Name'.

The rabbi will take pupils to see the holiest place in the synagogue, the ark, which is set on a raised platform called a *bimah* near the centre of the room. Explain that in Britain the congregation will face the ark while praying because this is facing East where Jerusalem is situated.

F Use **Copymaster 40** (Listen and answer) for children to raise and record simple questions and answers during their visit to the synagogue. They could ask the rabbi these questions:

- What is your name?
- What is the ark and how old is it?
- Why are the scrolls kept behind a curtain?
- What is the curtain made of?
- Why do Jewish people go to church on Saturdays and not on Sundays?
- How long does the Sabbath go on for?
- What happens at the Sabbath?
- Do a lot of people come to the synagogue?
- Why is a cap or *yarmulka* worn by boys and men?

These questions can be written on a separate sheet to accompany the copymaster. Pupils can then use all the space in the box to write down the rabbi's responses.

G Read the story **Jacob in the synagogue** (p. 49) to the class when you return from the synagogue.

The tallith *or prayer shawl*

H Look at pictures of Jews at prayer. Set a table in the classroom as if for a Sabbath meal with a special *challah* loaf from a Jewish bakery, a glass of wine and two Sabbath candles. Find out how many of the children remember the Fourth Commandment – to keep the Sabbath Day holy.

Invite girls to sit at the table. Tell the class that the Jewish holy day begins on Friday evening when the men and boys of the family go to the synagogue and women and girls stay at home. Then light the candles before the class, explaining that the mother of a family, as she is lighting the candles, may say, 'We ask God's blessing on

45

our family circle and we unite ourselves with the people of Israel in all lands and all ages as we kindle these Sabbath lights'.

Bring the boys to the table. Explain that the Father will place his hands on his sons' heads and say, 'God make you like Ephraim and Manassah'. He will then place his hands on the girls' heads and say, 'God prosper you and make you like Rachel and Leah'.

I Ask the children to sit very quietly and tell them that they are going back nearly 5 000 years to a desert town called Haren. Read the story **Jacob meets Rachel and Leah** (p. 50) which explains why the Jewish Sabbath prayer is for girls to become like Rachel and Leah. Afterwards, explain that Rachel's son, Joseph, had two sons, Ephraim and Manassah, who were loved by everyone, and that Jewish boys at the Sabbath are linked with Ephraim and Manassah in the hope that they will become more like them.

J Sit with the children at the table and hold a simple Sabbath meal. Discuss with them the way in which the following day, Saturday, and the main day of the Sabbath will be spent in Orthodox Jewish homes. Programme six 'Judaism' of Coming Together shows children talking about how they spend the Sabbath Day.

K Read the story **Naomi goes to the synagogue** (p. 50) and discuss the activities that take place there and what happens when she arrives home. Ask the children to make a list of the quiet activities Naomi will be able to take part in on the Sabbath.

L Make a model of the interior of a synagogue, using the completed copies of Copymaster 39 and putting in the holy ark, the *bimah*, the pews and the gallery.

TOPIC STORIES

The little donkey

The little donkey was sad. He was, in his opinion, quite old and strong enough to carry someone on his back or take the cart to the market in Jerusalem.

'Be thankful you don't have to work yet,' said his mother who often worked long hours pulling the cart or with heavy baskets strapped to their sides. 'Your turn will come, be patient.'

The older donkeys who shared the little donkey's stable in Bethany, a mile from Jerusalem, were not so kind.

'No one wants to ride you yet. You are too small and you'd probably cry all the time.'

'No, I wouldn't,' argued the little donkey. 'I'm getting bigger. We all have to start somewhere.'

One morning, a tall man came to the stables. The owner hurried to greet him. He obviously knew the stranger well.

'I'll be needing to hire a young donkey from you the day after the Sabbath – on Sunday,' said the tall man. 'It must be a donkey no one has ridden yet.'

'Yes, Lord. I have just the animal for you,' answered the owner. 'He's all by himself in the stable now. Come and see.'

The little donkey was so excited he could hardly breathe. Someone wanted to ride him. He pawed the ground and neighed happily. The tall stranger saw him and laughed.

'He'll do,' he said and he put a gentle hand on the donkey's head. 'You'll take me carefully into Jerusalem, won't you?' he said.

The little donkey felt he was a hundred feet tall. He liked this man and he would certainly carry him carefully.

When the stranger had gone, the owner of the stables came to see the donkey. He gave him a titbit and patted the donkey's grey head.

'Well done, little donkey,' he said. 'On Sunday you will be carrying a King.'

Of course the little donkey had to brag to the older ones but they pushed him out of the way impatiently.

'He's made it up because we said no one would want to ride him,' they said.

'I tell you, I'm going to carry a King,' shouted the donkey and his mother turned to him angrily.

'Don't tell lies,' she warned. 'I've told you that you'll be able to work soon. There's no need to make things up.'

The little donkey said nothing. He believed the tall stranger would come for him.

46

Sunday was a working day for the Jews and the little donkey was disappointed when his mother and the other donkeys set out early for the market. He had so much wanted them to see him carry the King. At last two men came to the stables. They asked the owner for the little donkey whom no one had ridden yet and soon the little donkey was outside the stable and being led away by a rope.

The two men were kind and the donkey had to stop himself from kicking his legs in the air with delight. Soon he would see his friend, the King, again. They reached a house at the foot of the steep hill leading up to Jerusalem. The tall stranger was waiting. He greeted the little donkey lovingly and then the great moment came. The tall man was on the donkey's back and urging him gently forward.

The hill up to the city was steep but the donkey managed to climb it, the tall stranger who was now his friend telling him how clever he was and that he could do it. The gates of Jerusalem were open and the donkey, his head held high, proudly trotted in. He did not expect such a welcome, and though the shouts and cheers were, he knew, for the King on his back, everyone cheered him, the donkey, as well. (He knew that.) Palm branches were waved and put on the ground for him to walk on and the donkey kept going, even though so many people tried to stop him.

As they rode past the market place, the little donkey saw his mother and the other donkeys swarmed around him.

They stopped for a short time at the temple and the little donkey was given food and water. Then the King came out and they went on their way again.

When the other donkeys returned to their stables that night they looked at the donkey with a new respect. His mother was especially proud.

'You see, he wasn't telling lies,' she told the other donkeys.

For a few days, the little donkey was happy but then he heard some terrible news. His mother had told him as gently as she could his King, the lovely man he had taken to Jerusalem was dead.

'He was a wonderful person but he had some enemies and they put him on a cross and killed him,' she said.

The little donkey cried himself to sleep. The next morning he could not understand why everyone, the other donkeys and even the owner were staring at him.

'Come out into the yard, little one,' said the owner. 'I want to take a look at you.'

Soon everyone seemed to be standing around the donkey. 'Mum,' he whispered, 'what is it?'

'You've got a cross on your back,' his mother said. 'It appeared in the night. You are an unusual donkey.'

The little donkey was special to everyone after that but he was only happy when he heard some wonderful news. The donkeys told him that the King – his King – had been seen by several people. He was thought to be alive.

The little donkey did not see his kind friend, the King, again, but he knew Jesus was alive and no one would ever doubt that he, the youngest donkey, had once carried a King. He had the symbol of the cross on his back to prove it.

The Prophet Muhammad

When the prophet Muhammad was a young man, he was so friendly and helpful that everyone called him 'The Trustworthy One'. A lot of the time Muhammad was away from Mecca, helping his uncle, Abu Bakr to sell camels and spices. Whenever he was in the city of Mecca he walked every day to the mosque, the most holy place of worship in all Arabia.

Muhammad went to the mosque to worship Allah who is God but he did not like all that was happening there. Hundreds of idols were found in the mosque, all of different gods. The people in charge of the Ka'aba, who were actually related to Muhammad, were charging visitors large sums of money, not just if they wished to pray to their idols or buy small statues but if they wanted a cup of water as well.

Muhammad knew this was wrong. There was only one God, Allah, not hundreds of others. The Prophet did not like to see pilgrims, some of them very poor, paying large sums of money when they had really come to the mosque to pray.

Many years later, when Muhammad became the ruler of Mecca, he walked to the mosque and swept all the idols from the shelves with his stick. By this time, most people worshipped one God, Allah and those who did not didn't dare to stop Muhammad from sweeping away the idols.

'Get rid of those idols,' he ordered. 'Now at last Muslims may worship freely and in peace.'

Ganesh

Ganesh is a much loved god. He brings good fortune and success. Hindus pray to him when they are hoping for an idea to work.

Lord Shiva and his wife, Parvati, had a son called Ganesh. One day, Parvati said to her son, 'I am going to have a bath. Listen carefully, Ganesh. You must not let anyone into the house until I come back. Promise me, my son.'

'I promise,' answered Ganesh and he kept his promise.

When Lord Shiva, his father, came home, Ganesh refused to open the door to him and when Lord Shiva managed to force his way into the house, he cut off Ganesh's head in a rage.

When Parvati appeared, she was horrified and she cried so much that Lord Shiva said, 'I will replace Ganesh's head with the head of the first creature who passes our door.'

The first animal to pass Shiva's door was an elephant and Shiva cut off its head and put it on Ganesh.

'Hindus must pray to Ganesh before they pray to anyone else,' Shiva said.

Seeva's story

I am Seeva and I was nearly seven years old when the white invaders came. We were peaceful people and we

47

never wanted to fight. We could defend ourselves when the enemy tribes sailed up the River Indus – we defended ourselves well until the white men came.

I was happy until then. We were all happy, my mother and father and my brothers and sisters sang as they went about their work and so did I. Once a week, if I helped on the farm, I could go to the big city to the granary and sell our produce – well, my brothers did that but I listened and watched because one day my father might send me to do the selling. My brothers always bought a small toy for me and one for my sister if the rice and vegetables sold well.

Then the white men came with all their weapons and they invaded our valley, putting themselves in charge of us. They were good warriors but they knew nothing about farming. Then they divided us all into four groups. First there were the priests. I didn't know what a priest was so I asked my father and he said, 'These people, the Aryans, they believe in a lot of gods and that everyone should worship these gods. The priests are in charge of how we should worship.'

'What do you mean, "Worship them"?' I asked.

'Pray to them, talk to them and ask for their help.'

My father didn't seem to be very sure. 'They have a god of storms, a god of fire and a sun god.'

The next group called themselves warriors. I knew what they were. They had invaded our valley and fought us. They were the soldiers. Then came the shopkeepers, the merchants who sold things. Last of all came the labourers.

'That's us,' said father, angrily. 'We have to work for the Aryans now. I have no farm to hand on to my sons. I have to pay rent to our invaders and give them some of our profits.'

Therefore, life changed in our peaceful valley.

'One day I shall be a warrior and I'll win the farm back for you, father,' I cried fiercely, and my father and brothers laughed at me but they weren't really making fun.

'Seeva, you can't do that. You can't join another group. You are a labourer and you'll always be a labourer like the rest of us.'

Then I understood. We'd been put into the groups, or castes as they called them, for ever. We could never change the new order of things.

Ram the priest
Ram is a Hindu priest in Calcutta, West Bengal. He gets up very early in the morning, usually at dawn and bathes thoroughly, putting on clean clothes. He will then make his way to the temple of Vishnu where he will remove his shoes and enter with his back to the sun. First he will see the vehicle of Vishnu, a large snake on which the god always rides. Ram will go up some steps to the central sanctuary and into the porch before arriving at the nave, the main part of the temple where the worshippers will sit on the floor.

Ram enters a small, dark room leading from the shrine room to wash and dress the images of the gods before the worshippers arrive. Before actually clothing the

gods, Ram will offer them flowers, incense and fruit. Music will be played to entertain the god.

Worshippers come to offer *bhakti* (devotion) by lighting a candle and saying prayers. As worshippers leave they are given *prashad* (sacred food offered to the gods). In the evening, Ram will offer food to the image again and bath the god before putting the image to bed.

Congregational acts of worship are in three parts. *Havan* (fire offering) means that the priest will use a portable fire altar to light the sacred fire. He will use wood, camphor and ghee. Parts of the Vedas, the sacred writings from Aryan times will be recited, such as 'Let us meditate upon the excellent light, our radiant sun, may he guide our minds'. The sacred fire represents the mouth of the god, eating the offerings in the smoke.

Ram will say prayers for purity and he will touch each part of his body as a sign of ceremonial washing as he says, 'Let my tongue have speaking power, my ears have the power of hearing, my nose inhaling power, and the eyes, seeing power. May my arms and thighs have strength and all the limbs be full of energy.' The *arti* ceremony (the worship of light) invites the use of a flat tray with five candles on it, representing the elements. This is waved in front of the shrine.

Incense and flowers representing the earth are presented at the same time. A fan is waved to represent air and a conch shell is sounded to stand for ether and water. Red paste is put on the foreheads of the statues of the gods before the arti dish is passed round for the people to pass their hands over their heads. The congregation receives God's blessing and power in this way. Bells, tambourines, triangles and other instruments accompany the singing of *bhajans* (hymns) which follow.

Prashad is given out and there will be readings from the *Bhavagad Gita* which Krishna gave to Hindus.

The last plague
Moses was a kind young man and he did not like to see the Israelites being badly treated by the Egyptian task masters.

One day, Moses saw an Egyptian being cruel to an Israelite. He killed the Egyptian and buried the man's body in the sand. When the King heard about this he sent his soldiers to arrest Moses. By this time Moses was on his way into the desert. He had managed to escape.

Moses stayed in the desert for 40 years. He married a girl called Zipparah and he and his wife had two sons. Moses worked as a shepherd and would have been happy to have stayed in the desert town of Midian all his life.

God had other plans for Moses. He spoke to Moses through a burning bush in the desert and told Moses to go back to Egypt and rescue the Israelites from the cruel King.

Moses returned to Egypt and when the King refused to let the Israelites go, God sent ten plagues to persuade him to change his mind. The River Nile ran with blood. There were flies, locusts, frogs. The people had boils and the animals became ill. Thunder and lightning frightened everyone and huge hailstones hurt the people as they fell.

It was the last plague which finally changed the King's mind. Moses told the Israelites that they should kill a lamb and paint their doorposts with its blood. They should prepare a special meal after they had packed their belongings. They must be ready to leave at a moment's notice.

The Angel of Death struck down the first born child of every Egyptian home from the King to his poorest subject, but passed over the homes of the Israelites. They were safe.

The escape

Part 1: Leaving Egypt

Ephraim was 7 years old when the messenger ran through the dark streets of Goshen, in the Israelite quarters of Egypt. For hours, all doors had been firmly closed because Moses, the great leader, had said that the Angel of Death would be passing over Israelite homes. Ephraim's family had been preparing the last meal they would ever eat in Egypt.

'There won't be time for the bread to rise, so don't put any yeast into it,' all Israelites had been told.

Ephraim looked now at the flat unleavened bread and the table with the food left out for them.

The old cart was ready outside but their belongings could not be put into it until the message came.

'We'll have to hurry,' Ephraim's father said, over and over again. 'We'll have to get out of Egypt as quickly as possible before the King changes his mind.'

'But we'll have our meal first,' said Rachel, Ephraim's mother, firmly. 'It could be many hours before we have fresh food to eat again and we must think of the children.'

The messenger could be heard, knocking on Israelite doors. 'Hurry, children of Israel. We must leave now. Load up your carts.'

For the first time in his life Ephraim ate a meal standing up. 'And don't fill your mouth too full,' ordered his mother, after the prayers had been said and they could eat. 'Do stand still, Ephraim.'

Ephraim tried not to choke on the pieces of lamb and the unleavened bread. He had to be patient as the cup of wine was passed round and as usual he had to dip his hands into clean water between the courses.

The family shared the cart and the ox with another family in the street and now it seemed that everyone was running non-stop, loading the carts, women and children helped into them, men alongside. As their cart left the streets of Goshen, Ephraim knew he would remember the scene for the rest of his life. Thousands of Israelites on the move, some in carts like theirs, others in covered wagons, some leading herds of sheep and goats. The noise was deafening, but exciting just the same.

They had left Egypt behind and were approaching the sea when something happened. Shouts and cries from the crowds made Ephraim stand up in the chart and grab his brothers and sisters in terror.

'The King has changed his mind. He's sent his soldiers after us in the war chariots. We'll all be killed!'

Screams and shouts followed as the carts and wagons crunched to a stop by the stormy water. Ephraim saw Moses, their leader, tall and stern, facing the angry crowds.

'Why didn't you leave us where we were in Egypt?'
'Now we will all die.'
'We've lost everything now.'

Ephraim saw Moses take the stick he always carried and raise it over the water. He seemed to be praying. Then shouts of wonder could be heard. The river suddenly opened, the waters in a huge bank on either side.

'God be praised and Moses too!' someone shouted and, in a great rush the carts and wagons and people and animals plunged on to the sea bed. Behind him – far behind him – the King's soldiers could be seen.

'They're coming across too,' said Ephraim, craning his neck to see above the thousands of travellers.

At last, everyone was across and the waters rolled back into place, drowning the Egyptian army. Ephraim stared around him. The cart was now being pulled across sand. They were in the desert. A new life lay ahead for them all.

'Ephraim, my son, you will never have to be a slave as I have been,' said the boy's father, lifting Ephraim out of the cart. 'You will be a free man – and we have Moses, our leader to thank for that because he was sent to us by God.'

Part 2: The Ten Commandments

When Ephraim was about 9 years old, the Israelites camped at the foot of Mount Sinai and Moses called everyone together. He said he was going to the top of the mountain to talk to God and he would come back with the rules which God wanted all his followers to keep.

At first everyone went on with their lives as usual. Ephraim was now big enough to help his father repair the cart and he could make the fire for the family to cook their meals. Fights would often break out in some of the groups sitting around campfires at night and Aaron, Moses' brother, tried to keep order.

'Moses will be back soon,' he kept saying, 'he won't be pleased to find you all fighting each other.'

No one took any notice. 'Moses will never come back,' the people shouted.

Moses did come back in the end and he brought with him ten very special rules or commandments which God had given him. They were written on stone tablets. Ephraim soon knew these by heart.

Jacob in the synagogue

Jacob wears the *yarmulka* all the time because he believes that an act of worship does not happen on the Sabbath Day only or when he attends the synagogue. Jacob believes that all life is worship and he tries to worship God in his whole life, not only at prayer times and on special occasions.

'We are under God's heaven all the time,' he says. Jacob sits in a special pew near to the *bimah*.

'My grandfather and my father had this pew before me,' explained Jacob. 'I took it over from them and I pay rent for it – a higher rent than many people because it is close to the *bimah*. Sometimes my young son and daughter sit with me in the pew and at other times they sit with my wife in the Women's Gallery.' Jacob laughs. 'It just depends really, whether I've been cross with my children and made them angry with me. But it is also because sometimes they like to sit up high on the gallery where they can see everything.'

Before praying, whether it is at home or in the synagogue, Jacob will put on a *tallith* or prayer shawl. The rings on the shawl will remind Jacob of the many commandments God has given which he must try to keep. Jacob will place the prayer shawl or *tallith* over his head and with his head covered completely, he will say:

'Even as I cover myself with the *tallith* in this world so may my soul deserve to be clothed with a beauteous spiritual robe in the world to come.'

Jacob will then place the shawl around his shoulders and say, 'Blessed art Thou, O lord God, King of the Universe, who has sanctified us by Thy commandments and has commanded us to enwrap ourselves in a fringed garment.'

Jacob meets Rachel and Leah

In the big tent across the fields Leah, Rachel's sister, was cooking the evening meal. Leah was not as pretty as Rachel and she was older. Laban, the girls' father, was sitting in the farmyard trying to work out how he could make more money.

'If only I'd had sons instead of daughters,' he muttered to himself. 'Someone who could help me to build up my flock of sheep.'

Rachel, dreaming in the fields, saw a young man walking towards her. He wasn't very tall and he had long, dark, curly hair and dark eyes.

'Hello,' he said, smiling at Rachel. 'Could you tell me how to find a farmer called Laban?'

'He's my father,' answered Rachel. 'Come with me. I'll take you to him.'

'What is your name?' asked the young man as he followed Rachel across the field.

'I'm Rachel,' she answered. 'Who are you?'

'My name is Jacob,' said the young man. 'We are cousins, Rachel. My mother is your father's sister.'

Rachel stared at Jacob. 'You are Aunty Rebekah and Uncle Isaac's son from Canaan?' she asked in surprise. 'You've come a long way.'

'Yes, I have, and I hope to be able to stay for a long time,' Jacob told her. 'Do you think Uncle Laban will let me stay?'

'Of course he will,' cried Rachel, as they stepped into the farmyard.

'Father,' she called. 'Where are you? We have a visitor.'

Laban looked up.

'Rachel, how many times have I told you not to talk to strangers?' he asked.

'I'm not really a stranger, Uncle Laban,' said Jacob quietly.

'What did you say?'

Laban stared at the young man. 'You called me "Uncle". Then you must be Rebekah's son. Which one?'

'I'm Jacob.' Jacob smiled at his Uncle. 'My mother has sent you a letter.'

He pulled a piece of parchment from his cloak and handed it to Laban who smoothed it carefully before reading it. Then the farmer nodded.

'You can stay here as long as you like,' he said. 'My name is yours now.'

Laban and Jacob hugged each other. Then Leah, her face hot from the cooking she had been doing, hurried out of the tent.

'Leah, my older daughter,' Laban said proudly. 'She keeps house for us and she's good at it, too.'

Jacob married first Leah, then Rachel. Both women were wives and friends to Jacob. This is why the Jewish Sabbath prayer is for girls to become like Leah and Rachel.

Naomi goes to the synagogue

Naomi is 7 years old and every Saturday she, her parents and her elder sister and brother, Hannah and Joseph, go to the synagogue, a mile from their home, for the Sabbath service.

When they arrive at the synagogue, Naomi's father and her brother go into the downstairs area and Naomi goes upstairs with her mother and Hannah to sit in the gallery.

Naomi likes the synagogue. It is big and colourful and it has beautiful windows stained in blue and red. She likes to watch her father and brother wearing their white silk *talliths* (shawls) with patterns on them. Naomi remembers how proud Joseph was when he wore his shawl for the first time. She likes the tassels on the shawl best of all.

Joseph and her father are wearing their *yarmulkas* too, patterned caps which Jewish men must wear when they pray. Her father's cap is black and Joseph's is white with a pattern on it.

Naomi can see the holy ark from where she is sitting. She knows how precious and holy the ark is to all Jews. The ark in her synagogue has doors and a curtain and is made of marble, with five domes on top. It is painted in bright colours with pillars at the side. The domes on the top have six painted stars on them and Naomi knows this is the Jewish symbol, the Star of David.

The best moment in the service for Naomi is when the Torah is carried around the synagogue and as it passes the men lean forward to touch the Torah's mantle with the hem of their prayer shawl, which they then kiss. This is done, Naomi knows, because the Torah contains the word of God and is treated with great respect.

The parchment of the Torah must not be touched by human hands so when it is being used a *yad*, a silver pointer, is used to follow the text.

When the service is over, Naomi and her family will greet their friends outside the synagogue and then they will make their way home. No work of any kind must be done on the Sabbath but Naomi is allowed to read, play quiet games or play with her toys. The Sabbath will end on Saturday evening at sunset when the family will pray together before the ordinary week begins.

Prayers will still take place in Naomi's home. On the upper right doorposts of Jewish homes are small containers called *mezzuzah*s. They are found on the inside and outside of Jewish houses (instructions by God to put them there are found in Deuteronomy 6:9; 11:20). Inside the *mezzuzah* is a piece of parchment on which is written the *shema*, a Hebrew prayer. The word *shema* means 'hear' and the prayer is 'Hear, O Israel. The Lord your God is One and you shall love the Lord your God with all your heart and with all your soul and with all your might.'

Naomi's family also feel that the *mezzuzah* will help to protect their home as well as helping them to remember God's Law. Every Jewish person will touch or kiss the *mezzuzah* as they pass.

Beliefs and lifestyles

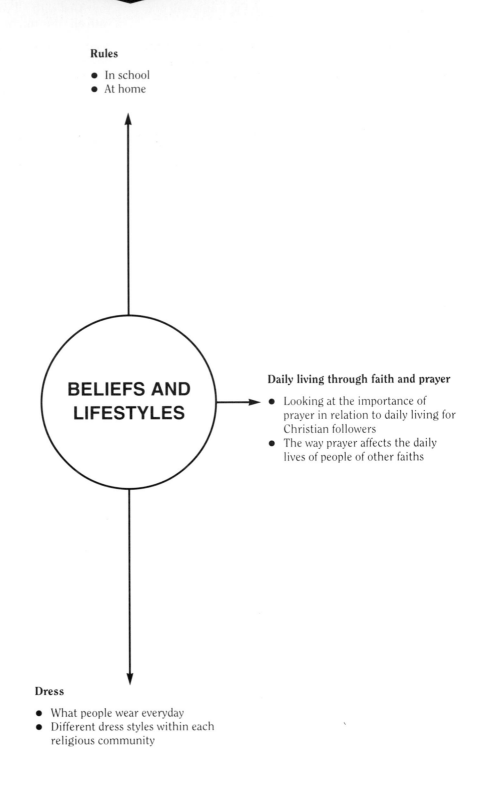

Rules
- In school
- At home

BELIEFS AND LIFESTYLES

Daily living through faith and prayer
- Looking at the importance of prayer in relation to daily living for Christian followers
- The way prayer affects the daily lives of people of other faiths

Dress
- What people wear everyday
- Different dress styles within each religious community

LEARNING OBJECTIVES

- To be aware of rules which are necessary for living (home, school, public and personal safety).
- To consider the importance of dress for different occasions and especially in religious ceremonies.
- To become aware that some people's lives are directed and influenced by rules and customs which are part of their religious beliefs and practices.
- To be able to recognise the symbols for at least three religious traditions, and to be aware of rules affecting the lifestyles of the adherents of the faiths concerned.
- To be aware of religious stories which give guidance concerning rules for living.

STARTING POINTS

- Ask the children to give examples of school rules they learnt. List them on the blackboard or a flipchart. Ask the children if they have ever thought about why the school has rules that they must keep to and why they are needed.

- The children can write down other rules for school that they think would be helpful to everybody.

- Ask the children to write down examples of rules that they must keep at home, thinking about why there must be such rules while they do this. How helpful is it to have rules at home?

- Ask the class to recite the Green Cross Code altogether. Make a class poster for the wall with the words of the Green Cross Code in the middle and place pictures depicting the code being carried out around the outside. Ask the children why they think we have a Green Cross Code.

- Can the children think of any rules that religious people obey? Write some of their suggestions down on the blackboard.

- Learn and sing together the topic song, **I believe**.

RULES

Area of study 1

Purpose

To look at rules that exist at school and in the home and how their existence affects our lives.

Activity 1: Rules at school

A Sit the children informally and show them a photograph of their school. They should immediately recognise it. Ask them if they know how many children are in their school. When they have told you this or you have told them, remind them that all the children in school have to have a set of rules which they must follow. Ask them why they think this is necessary. Could they imagine school being a happy place in which to work and have friends if there were no rules? They should agree that a set of rules makes life in school easier and more enjoyable for everyone.

✔ Ask the children if they can remember any school rules and use **Copymaster 41** (My school rules) to write them out neatly, using a different coloured crayon for each school rule so that they all stand out on the page. (Leave the 'Reasons' column blank for the moment.)

The children can then talk about the rules, working

out together why they have been chosen. Talk to the class as a whole about the rules. Choose a rule that demonstrates practical commonsense such as 'No running down the corridors'. Ask the children to explain why this rule has been chosen. Then select a rule where the right attitude needs to be put into practice. This might be 'Always say please and thank you to your teacher and friends'. Continue to discuss other rules with the children, drawing from them the conclusion that all the rules in school are there for a good reason, and they must remember this when they put them into practice.

Returning to the copymaster, tell pupils to look at the rules again and this time in the space provided, write down the reason why they think each school rule exists.

B Show the children an old photograph of a school classroom in Victorian times. Compare school life then and now with them: notice the furniture (benches nailed to the floor) and the lack of displays on the walls and ask the class how the children in the picture are sitting at their desks. Are they leaning over or sitting upright? What was the school rule in those days, do they think, about how they sit at their desk? Explain to them that there were other rules for the classroom too, like not wandering out of their bench seats at any time: the teacher was the only person who was allowed to walk around the room freely. Examine the expressions on pupils' faces. Are they looking happy? If not, why not? Do pupils think that because school life in those days was so strict with so many rules to follow, the children did not enjoy themselves at school? Why?

C Borrow books on school in Victorian times from the library. Ask the children to look up and make a list of rules that had to be obeyed at school in those days. Ask them if they think these rules stopped the children from enjoying themselves. How? Do their own school rules do this? Discuss the differences. Look at a photograph of a present-day class in the school (preferably one of their own class) and talk about the differences in expression. Why do they think the children in the photograph look happier?

D Pupils can write a short description about being in school today and why it is important and necessary to obey school rules if we are to make being in school an enjoyable experience.

E Invite pupils to act out a play, scene one taking place in Victorian times and scene two in the present day. Bring out the harsher attitudes of the lifestyle of times past, and the many practical rules that had to be obeyed in the classroom and in school as a whole. Prepare a simplified version of a short extract from Dickens' *David Copperfield* and read it to the children to help them with characterisation.

F The children can write a poem called 'My school is . . .' describing what they like about it and how and why it is a good place in which to be. Alternatively, pupils can draw pictures of themselves putting their school rules into practice and underneath write about what rules they have depicted and why they are a good idea.

Activity 2: Rules at home
A Discuss with the children what rules they have in their home.

✓ Give out **Copymaster 42** (At home, do I . . . ?) and read the rules with the children to help them. They should fill in the first column with the word 'yes' or 'no', then take the copymaster home and ask the person who looks after them to make any comments in the final column. This column shows whether the children's answers have been accurately recorded by them. A note can be sent home with the copymaster explaining to parents that they might like to qualify any of the 'rules' given to correspond more accurately to their family's lifestyle and beliefs. When all the copymasters have been returned a bar graph can be made to show which rules are most widely practised in their homes.

B The children can draw pictures of the activities that they do to help life in the home to be more enjoyable and easier for their Mum or Dad.

C Tell the class that you are going to read them a set of rules that are followed by many other children and people around the world. Explain that they were given by God to Moses on a mountain called Sinai (write this name on the board) many years ago. Now read **The Ten Commandments** (p. 60) slowly to the class. Children can bring out the cards they have made (see **Worship**, Copymaster 38) and revise them.

Do the children notice any similarities between the Ten Commandments and the rules they are expected to follow at school and at home, in everyday life? Select ten pupils and invite each one to write one of the Commandments on the board. Then ask another ten pupils to write down an equivalent rule beside each Commandment: thus 'Thou shalt not steal' in the first column becomes 'Never take anything that belongs to somebody else' in the second.

D The children can write a simple poem called, 'I must, I must' consisting of two verses. Ask them to think carefully about the rules they have learnt as they write the poem. They can draw a decorative border around their poem and colour it in.

DAILY LIVING THROUGH FAITH AND PRAYER

C43

Purpose

To examine how people with faith try to live their daily lives.

Activity 1: Christian prayer and daily living

A Play the children a recording of a sung version of the Lord's Prayer. Ideally this should be in modern style so that the words are easier for the children to understand. Programme Two, 'A Surprise Death', of *Coming Together* shows a family enjoying themselves in the country on a bright, sunny day over which the Lord's Prayer is heard. The film draws a parallel between the role of father in the family and the Christian belief of God, the Loving Father, who looks after us.

B Talk about God sending his Son, Jesus, to earth and how he taught us to say the Lord's Prayer, to guide us in our everyday lives. Point out that Christians who follow Jesus say this prayer and attempt to put into practice what it tells us to do.

Give the children a copy of the words of the Lord's Prayer and read it through with them. Ask them to tell you what the prayer is saying about how to live our daily lives. Highlight the words 'forgive' and 'temptation'. Write them down on the blackboard and ask the children what these words mean.

C Divide the class into groups. Give each group a situation in which they might find themselves where they are tempted to do something or where they are forgiven in some way. For example, Janet might share a secret with her friend Naomi and she asks her friend not to tell anybody, but Naomi is tempted to tell Patty and does so. Janet finds out her friend has not kept the secret and has to forgive her for this, so that they can remain good friends. Ask the group to act out this situation, bringing out Janet's feelings of hurt as she trusted Naomi and the forgiveness she showed her at the end of the scene.

Another example would be a scene where a boy sees a lovely pen on his teacher's desk. The teacher is busy mounting work on the classroom wall. The boy is tempted to steal the pen as it is just what he has always wanted, and he puts it in his pocket. Some time later, the teacher notices the pen is missing and questions the class. She discovers who has taken it and explains she has to punish him for this, but also explains to the class that it is best to forget about the whole incident and pretend it has not happened. Say that this is her way of forgiving the boy and we must all forgive each other for doing wrong to each other.

The groups can role-play their scenes based upon the wording of the Lord's Prayer. Discuss the scenes afterwards together, emphasising that the children have been looking at examples of how to live their lives in the right way – the way Jesus himself recommended when he taught us the Lord's Prayer. Explain that Jesus taught his followers to pray to him and ask for help

whenever they found themselves in difficult situations in everyday life, like the ones they have just acted out in front of each other.

D Pupils can look up stories in the Bible telling of people prayed to God in difficult times and he answered their prayers. They can draw pictures of the stories chosen underneath a brief description of the story.

E Ask the children to write their own prayers on themes they have read about and others like 'sadness', 'joy', 'loneliness', 'thankfulness' and so on, bringing out their own personal feelings. They can illustrate their prayers, by perhaps drawing a picture of themselves praying.

The prayers can then be mounted on the classroom wall and the title 'Our prayers' should be placed above them.

Activity 2: Prayer and its effects on the daily lives of people of other faiths

A Tell the children that so far you have been looking at how Christians believe that praying to God in their everyday lives helps them to try to live a good life, and you are now going to all look at how believers of other faiths pray in their everyday lives.

B Show the children a picture of a group of Muslims at prayer. Remind them that these people follow a faith called Islam and pray to their one God called Allah. Write this name on the blackboard. Muslims believe they must pray to Allah five times a day.

white overshirt

white cap

no shoes

prayer mat

Write the words 'In the name of Allah, the most merciful, the most kind' and ask the children to recite this aloud from the blackboard or flipchart. Tell them that this is the beginning of a Muslim prayer which is said no less than 17 times a day. Explain that Muslims pay respect to Allah through prayer. Discuss the meaning of the word 'respect' and what 'paying respect to God' actually means to people when praying.

C Show the children a Muslim prayer mat, and say that as a sign of respect to God, they use this so as not to

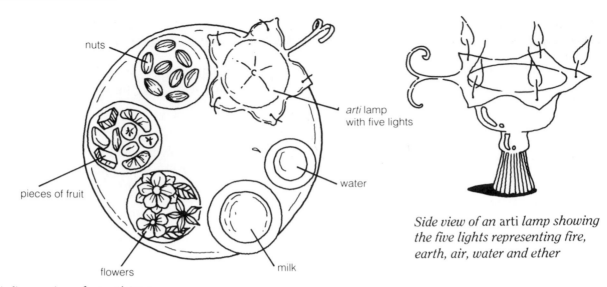

Side view of an arti *lamp showing the five lights representing fire, earth, air, water and ether*

Bird's eye view of an arti *tray*

let their bodies touch the ground. Explain that Muslims also always wash, remove their shoes and cover their heads before praying. Ask the children why they think these particular acts are important to Muslims.

D Tell the class you are going to show them other important objects used in prayer, only this time they are used by Hindu worshippers.

E Show them an *arti* or *puja* tray. Tell them what it is called, writing its name on the blackboard. Can they recognise what is on the tray (fruit, flowers, nuts, milk, water). Tell the children that this tray is used both in the home and in the temple as Hindus pray and worship. Write the word *puja* on the board and tell them that this is their word for 'prayers'. Explain that the *arti* prayer is the one most commonly used by Hindu worshippers and during this important time of prayer and worship they offer food and commit themselves totally to God.

Obtain an *arti* lamp and ask the children how many lights there are on it. Light the five lights and carefully wave the lamp in a circular motion to demonstrate how it is used in front of the image of their god. Remind the children of their work on the images of Hindu gods (see **Worship**, p. 42).

Now play a recording of Indian music that would be sung at this time and explain that the worshippers clap their hands as they sing praises to their god, asking for his guidance in their everyday lives.

If possible, ask the Education Officer at the local Hindu temple to come into school and talk to the children about the *arti* ceremony that takes place in the temple. If this is not possible, watch Programme Two of *Coming Together* which demonstrates the *arti* ceremony in the home.

F Brainstorm the class to find out what they remember about the Sikh faith. Then show them a picture of Sikh worshippers at prayer, mentioning that they too have a daily prayer called *mul mantra*. Write these words down on the blackboard. Read the prayer to the children and explain that Sikh followers show

respect to their 'one god' by saying this prayer which describes their god as 'creator of all things'.

Tell the children that Sikhs also pray to the Guru Granth Sahib, their holy book and, they believe, their present guru or teacher.

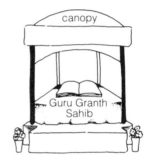

usually covered in prayer hall

Say out loud altogether the word 'Waheguru!' Tell pupils that after prayer worshippers always say this word which means 'Wonderful Lord'. Children can then draw a Sikh follower at prayer, writing the word 'Waheguru' underneath to remind themselves that this is what will be said after prayers have finished.

G Remind the class of their visit to a Jewish synagogue (see **Worship**, p. 44). Can they remember the name of the minister who leads prayer and worship there (a rabbi)?

Write the word 'Talmud' on the board and tell them that the rabbi reads from this book which is a collection of writings from other rabbis based on teachings from the Bible. Pass a Bible around the class and say this is an important part of Jewish worship. People believe they must think about God and reserve one day each week for him thus following the instruction given to Moses.

H Children can draw figure outlines of a rabbi and Moses in their workbooks. Within each figure they should write words and phrases associated with their roles in the Jewish faith.

I Read and discuss the stories **Jesus grows up** and **Jesus' Bar Mitzvah** (p. 61).

I Show the children an orange. Tell them the colour of the orange is very important to followers of a man called Buddha (hold up a picture of him with his name printed underneath or obtain a miniature statue). Say that these people are known as Buddhists and write this word down. Show the children a photograph of Buddhist followers sitting in a Buddhist temple, meditating. Ask the class what they think these people are doing and explain that followers of the Buddha spend many hours thinking deep thoughts about how to live in peace.

J Write down the Noble Eightfold Path on the blackboard and as you write it, talk to the children about how Buddhists try to live their lives through these words that they believe the Buddha gave them to follow. The children can copy the Noble Eightfold Path down on to a poster-size piece of paper, writing each line in a different colour so each stands out. At the foot of the poster they can draw their own picture of the Buddha and underneath write the words, 'To the Buddha, the *dharma* (duty) and the *sangha* (followers)', which should be explained to them.

K The children could write a letter and invite a member of the nearest Buddhist community to come into school and talk to them about their way of life.

L Summarise this Area of Study by discussing the faiths pupils have looked at. What do all these faiths have in common to enable us all to lead good, daily lives? Ask them to think of some words like 'peace', 'thoughtfulness', 'helpfulness' and 'kindness' and suggest to them that prayer helps everyone, whatever their faith, to think carefully about their lives and the way they should be lived.

The children can write some prayers of their own, thanking God for their lives and asking for guidance to lead good and happy lives every day. Pupils can record their prayers on to cassette and listen to each other's work. Alternatively, they could write a class prayer, beginning with the words 'Please God, whatever our faith is, we come together in prayer to ask you to help us be . . .', listing words like 'sharing', 'kind', 'caring', and so on, and thanking God at the end for listening.

M Use **Copymaster 43** (Prayer objects) which shows different objects used at prayer time. In the grid in the bottom right-hand corner of the copymaster, the children have to write the correct letter next to the faith to which the prayer object belongs.

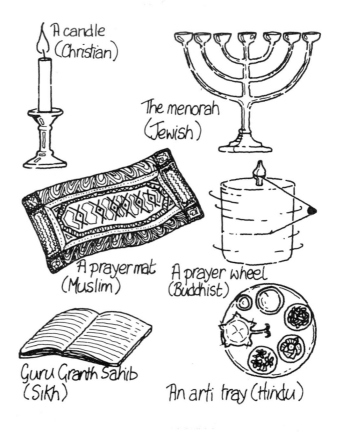

A candle (Christian)

The menorah (Jewish)

A prayer mat (Muslim)

A prayer wheel (Buddhist)

Guru Granth Sahib (Sikh)

An arti tray (Hindu)

Area of study 3

DRESS

C44 –50

Purpose
To look at everyday dress and the dress worn by believers for worship.

Activity 1: What people wear everyday
A Sit with the children informally and ask them to discuss the idea of a school uniform (whether there is a uniform worn in school or not). Do they think school uniform is a good idea and that everyone should look the same? If so, why? List on the blackboard their reasons for or against the idea of wearing school uniform.

B Show the children colour pictures of a police officer, a nurse, a firefighter, a religious minister. Ask them to identify these people and how they know what job they do. Ask them why these people have to wear a uniform (for example, practically safe and durable) and how does this help us, the public (easily recognisable).

C Use **Copymaster 44** (Uniforms for work) where children have to recognise the people from our community and fill in their job below the picture. The fifth box has been left blank for the children to draw another person who wears a uniform in their community and write their name in the space provided. The children can then colour in the pictures, cut them out and make a booklet of uniforms.

D Provide a wide variety of magazines and catalogues that contain different clothes we would wear everyday. Ask them to choose and cut out clothes that they would have liked to buy themselves and stick them on to a

large piece of paper, describing the appearance of the clothes underneath and why they like them.

E A large bar graph can be compiled, showing the number of children in the class and different types of clothes they would wear regularly, such as trousers, jeans, shorts, T-shirts, jumpers, shell suits, trainers, shoes, etc.

Work out which type of dress the children would wear regularly and like wearing and fill in the graph with them. Calculate which is the most popular style of dress and which type of dress the children would rather not wear, writing down the results on a record sheet next to the graph, which has been mounted on the classroom wall.

F Give out **Copymasters 45** and **46** (Clothes 1 and 2) and invite the children to draw themselves in clothes they would wear on the four suggested occasions, labelling each item of clothing. Afterwards they can cut out the pictures and make a clothes concertina, writing a few sentences underneath each picture explaining why they had chosen the clothes they had drawn.

G Look together at photographs of clothes worn on different occasions by the children. Start by looking at photographs of some of them at a birthday party celebration. Ask the children to describe the clothes and then draw themselves in what they were wearing in the photographs, saying why they had chosen their outfits and what they particularly liked about them. Discuss with them why they felt they wanted to dress up in these clothes and link this with the idea of celebration clothes. Examine special occasions such as weddings and christenings and discuss what is worn then you could bring in a christening robe, or bridal accessories for pupils to handle and describe.

H Collect together as many varieties of material that are available and pass them around the class. Consider the colour, texture and general effect that may be created when the material is used to make an item of clothing.

Now use **Copymaster 47** (My materials card) to make a materials card. Place the copymaster on to a piece of stiff card and stick it down. On it the children can arrange different materials they like and name the type of material and the sort of clothes for which the material may be suitable.

I Give each child a different piece of patterned material and ask them to look at the sample closely. They can then paint a picture copying the pattern and colour it as accurately as they can on to art paper. Tell them to cover the whole sheet of paper with the pattern. Mount all the pictures on the wall, edge to edge, and look at the effect created with the children and talk about it with them. Find out which patterns they think are most effective and why, talking about the shape and colour used in them.

Activity 2: Comparing dress styles of religious communities

A Introduce different dress styles within each religious community by sitting the children in an informal setting and showing them the Bible, explaining that there are stories within this book that mention clothes and that when these stories were written, people dressed very differently. Remind them of the robes they wore when acting out their Christmas stories (see **Birth celebrations**, p. 20). What does this style of dress tell us about the people who lived at the time of Jesus?

B Explain to the children that there is a story in the Bible about a little boy who was given a very special item of clothing by his father: it was a beautiful coat of many colours. Tell them this story can be found in the first part of the Bible called the Old Testament and ask the children to listen carefully as you read them the story of the boy Joseph (Genesis 37:1–36), whose life changed after he had received his amazing technicolour dreamcoat. Tell them they must describe to you after the story what happened to Joseph.

They can then draw a picture of Joseph in his coloured coat and listen to the song describing all the colours in it from *Joseph and his Amazing Technicolour Dreamcoat* while they are drawing it, so they can make sure they put all the right colours into the picture.

Study the clothes that were worn in the days when Joseph existed. Provide the children with sheets, striped materials, ropes for waistbands and sandals for their feet and ask them to dress up in the clothes. They can 'model' the clothes in front of each other and describe what they are wearing, giving themselves a character name and saying what job they do (a shepherd, a carpenter, a market seller, etc.).

C Explain to the children that people of different faiths like to dress up when they worship. Ask them why they think this is, and suggest that it is mark of respect to God to worship in clean, decent clothes. Tell them that together you are going to look at the way people dress within the religious communities in their local area.

First, show them photograph of a local church. Ask them to imagine what the congregation would look like who might be inside the church, worshipping God. Show them a clip from the television *Songs of Praise* programme when the camera scans down the rows of people singing hymns and afterwards ask the children if they noticed what the people were wearing. Did they all have the same style of dress on? Did they look smart? Why?

Mention the tradition of wearing an Easter bonnet in church on Easter Sunday and ask pupils why they think this is important at this time. You may like to help the children to make Easter bonnets out of card, ribbon and tissue paper.

If they were going to church themselves on a Sunday morning what would they wear? They can draw a special outfit and describe why they have chosen the clothes they have drawn underneath the picture. Discuss this choice of clothing afterwards with them.

D Give the children a long roll of crepe paper. Ask several children to hold the length of paper across the classroom and they will be amazed at how long the paper is. They will be even more amazed when you explain that men who follow a faith called Sikhism wear a turban on their heads which is this long. Tell the children that Sikhs have five parts to their uniform and

these are called the Five Ks. Show them the parts of the uniform which make a Sikh follower instantly recognisable, beginning with uncut hair called *kesh* (show a photograph), shorts called *kacha*, a bangle called *kara*, a small wooden comb called *khanga* and a short sword called *kirpan*.

Ask the children to write down their own description of the Five Ks from what you have shown and told them, noting why they are important to a Sikh follower.

E Show the children a picture of a Hindu man in traditional Western clothes. Tell them that Hindu men wear Western clothes every day. Then show the children a *sari* and ask them if they have seen these worn by some women in their local area. Tell the children the name of this garment and write it down on the blackboard. They can see for themselves the vast length of material required to make up the *sari*. Tell the children that just one piece of cloth is used as they can see, the length being five to eight metres and the width between 100 and 140 centimetres. Measure it with a metre ruler.

Explain that in the Hindu temple, the women often sit cross-legged on the floor to sing praises to their god in their *saris*, but praises can also be given standing up. Tell the children that worship and prayers in the temple are offered in a spirit of warmth, freedom and togetherness as these people worship.

F Show the children a picture of a woman in Muslim dress and ask them what faith she follows. Say that all members of Muslim families take their faith very seriously but it is probably the Muslim women in our local area who are most noticeable by the way they dress. Show the children a typical modest outfit worn by them pointing out the baggy trousers which are tight at the ankle (*shalwar*), the overdress to just below the knee (*kameez*) and the scarf (*dupatti*) which most women wear whenever they leave the house.

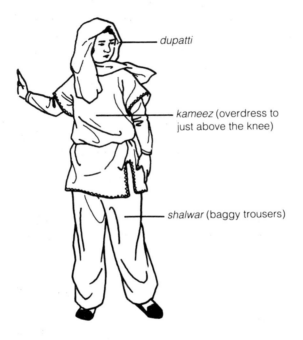

- dupatti
- kameez (overdress to just above the knee)
- shalwar (baggy trousers)

Write the words *shalwar* and *kameez* on card and place by the article of clothing. Say that Muslim men normally wear Western clothes but on special occasions they can be seen walking down the street towards the mosque or place of worship wearing a seamless white shirt and a white cap. Mention that Muslim women and girls on special occasions may decorate their forearms and hands with an orange dye called *henna* and may do this as part of their celebration called Eid-ul-Fitr, a time of rejoicing after the month of Ramadan when Muslims fast (remind them what this means) or drink between sunrise and sunset. Write the words *henna*, Eid-ul-Fitr and Ramadan on the blackboard.

G Show the children some photographs or pictures of Buddhist monks processing together around a monastery and ask them to tell you what they are wearing. Point out that Buddhists believe in wearing the simplest and most modest robes in which to worship, not attaching any importance to clothes but instead to thinking about life and a peaceful existence. Tell the children that their robes are a special orange colour called saffron and they fall gracefully to the floor.

H To conclude this section, arrange a row of pictures showing people going to worship, dressed in the clothes you have looked at. Mount them next to each other on the classroom wall and write the name of the faiths the people follow above each picture.

Distribute **Copymaster 48** (Community Clothes 1) and discuss the pictures with the children. Who are the people and what are they wearing? Ask them if they know which community the people belong to. The children can colour and cut out the pictures. Give out **Copymaster 49** (Community Clothes 2) and read the sentences with the children. They should fill in the gaps in the sentences with the names of the religions and clothes listed on the copymaster and then cut out each sentence. On a large piece of black sugar paper, the children can mount their pictures from Copymaster 48 and place the sentences underneath.

I To finish, show the children the world map on **Copymaster 50** (World believers) and discover with them where believers of the world originally came from, marking places on the map with coloured pins. Point out that people from different countries dress differently and when some left their original country to live in Britain they brought their beliefs and lifestyles with them.

TOPIC STORIES ▶

The Ten Commandments
The Israelites were not especially orderly or well behaved. They had been slaves for a very long time and most of them remembered nothing else but slavery and working from morning until night with hardly any pay. Therefore they argued, grumbled, fought and even killed each other and stole each other's belongings.

Moses knew the time had come for God to give the people some rules to live by. He left the people at the foot of Mount Sinai and climbed to the top of the mountain. The people could not see Moses any longer because he was hidden by a large cloud.

God spoke with Moses on the mountain top and gave him ten main rules for people to live by as well as a lot of other advice and rules. The ten main ones were known as the Ten Commandments:

1 I am the Lord, your God
2 You must not have any other gods before me
3 Don't take the name of the Lord your God in vain

4   Remember to keep the Sabbath Day holy
5   Honour your mother and your father
6   Don't kill anyone
7   Don't commit adultery
8   Don't steal
9   Don't bear false witness against your neighbour
10   Don't be envious of anything belonging to someone else.

Jesus grows up

Jesus grew up in Palestine 2000 years ago. He was brought up as a Jew.

Everyone in Palestine got up about 5 a.m. when the sun rose. Mary, Jesus' mother, would do her housework at that time and Joseph would begin work in his shop. It was the coolest part of the day and the best time for getting work done.

Jesus might have liked to watch Mary mixing the dough and baking the bread. Their bread was like large thick pancakes.

Jesus and his friends would play around the flat-roofed houses or wander through the market listening to the stall holders arguing over prices. The market would sell fruit, eggs, fish, clay pots, sandals, clothes and baskets.

Jesus liked holidays just as much as we do. He looked forward to the Holiday of Tents in September when everyone made a tent on the roof and camped in it for a week and there were lots of parties. Jesus remembered how good God had been to them in giving them a place to live.

Around December was the Holiday of Lights when everyone lit lamps and candles to remind themselves that God is always with us. Parties were held in many houses.

In April, Jesus, when he was old enough, walked 85 miles to Jerusalem with his family for the Passover Festival, when all Jews remember the rescue of the Israelite slaves from Egypt by Moses.

Jesus' Bar Mitzvah

When Jesus was 12, he became a grown-up in Jewish law. He had to stand up in the synagogue, read a passage from the scriptures and answer questions put to him by the learned teachers. He was given his prayer shawl for the first time and afterwards he went home to a great party, with food, wine and happy singing. This special event was called Bar Mitzvah and Jewish boys and girls have the same event today.

For Jesus, being Bar Mitzvah meant that he could go to the big city of Jerusalem for the Passover Festival. It was an 80-mile walk to Jerusalem and whole villages walked together by day and camped at night. It took three days to reach Jerusalem.

When the time came for Mary and Joseph to leave again they couldn't find Jesus, but thought he must be with other children and he would be back with them that night. When Jesus did not come, Joseph went to ask if anyone had seen Jesus. No one had seen him.

In the end, Mary and Joseph had to go all the way back to Jerusalem and begin the search there. They didn't find Jesus for three days. At Passover time, the clever men from the temple sat in the courtyard of the large temple answering questions put to them by all the visitors. Mary and Joseph saw that Jesus was sitting among these men. He was answering questions, not asking them and the learned men could not believe that a young boy could know so much.

Mary was not pleased at all and asked Jesus why he was behaving in such a way. Jesus answered that he had to do his Father's work.

The unhappy pig
(Can be read at any point throughout the topic)
When the school holidays arrive, many girls and boys are happy and excited but after a while they say to their mother, 'It's boring. I've nothing to do.' Some mothers might say, 'Well, if you are bored, you can clean your bedroom,' or find something for the boy or girl to do. (Most children will find something of their own to do after that in case their mothers think of other jobs for them to do.)

Willie, the white pig was bored. He lived by himself in a pretty cottage in a village where animals lived by themselves. Willie loved gardening and his garden was so beautiful that everyone stopped to admire it. His flowers, plants and vegetables often won prizes at shows all over the country.

Willie was getting bored, though. 'There must be easier ways of earning a living than digging in my garden and growing flowers and vegetables,' he thought to himself. 'It's hard work.'

A few days later, Willie locked his cottage door and set off to find a better job. He went first to the diary where Dennis, a big brown dog was standing by a large milk churn, pushing a pole up and down. Willie loved the cheese which Dennis sold to him every Friday and thought it must be easy to make. He knocked on the door of the dairy and Dennis told him to enter.
'Hello, Willie. Why aren't you working in your garden at this hour of the day?' asked Dennis, still pushing the pole up and down in the milk.
'I'm bored with being a gardener,' answered Willie. 'I'd like to make cheese like you. Will you show me how to do it?'
'Yes, of course,' replied Dennis. 'Take this pole and push it up and down until the cheese is made.'
Willie took the pole and began to move it up and down in the milk. After a while his arms grew tired and he stopped for a rest.
'Oh, you mustn't stop,' cried Dennis. 'You'll spoil the cheese. You must keep going.'
'I can't do it any more. My arms are too tired,' gasped Willie.
'I don't want to make cheese after all.' He gave the pole back to the dog and hurried out.

Further along the road he saw the ginger cat's cottage. Beautiful music was flowing out of it because Ginger played the fiddle and everyone loved to dance to his music.

'You make a good living out of playing the fiddle, don't you, Ginger?' asked Willie.

'Yes, I do,' answered Ginger. 'Why do you ask, Willie?'

'I want you to teach me how to play,' explained Willie. 'I'm bored with gardening. I want to do something else.'

'I'll teach you,' said Ginger. 'Here – take the fiddle and the bow and try.'

Willie took the fiddle and the bow but when he tried to play the fiddle made a terrible noise.

'Oh, don't worry. Everyone sounds like that at first,' smiled Ginger. 'Practise for five hours a day for a few years and you'll be able to play the fiddle well enough to earn your living.'

'Five hours a day for a few years?' cried Willie. 'Oh, no thanks. I can't do that.'

Mr Busy, the Bee Keeper, was taking honey from his beehives when Willie appeared.

'That honey looks good,' said Willie.

'Oh, it is,' answered Mr Busy. 'You know it is. I sell it to you every week.'

'Will you teach me to keep bees?' asked Willie. 'I'm bored with gardening.'

'Yes, I'll teach you,' answered Mr Busy, 'but you'll have to wear gloves and put a veil over your head and shoulders.'

Willie nodded and put on the veil and the gloves.

'Now, take the honeycomb,' said Mr Busy.

Willie bent down to pick it up. The bees suddenly swarmed all over him, getting into his veil and gloves and stinging him viciously. Willie screamed, dropped the gloves and veil and ran as fast as his legs would carry him.

Mr Busy shouted after him, 'Come back and try again. Everyone gets stung at first.'

'No, thank you,' Willie yelled back. 'I'm going back to my garden. It's safer.'

Later that day, a sadder and wiser pig was found in his garden as usual.

'Gardening is what I will do for now on,' Willie thought to himself. 'I know I want to go on doing it now. Everything else is too hard.'

Willie knew that all the jobs he had tried needed the same skills and patience but gardening was something he did well and he never tried to change his job again.

Sacred books

How books are important to us

- Looking at books we know
- Looking at library books

The Guru Granth Sahib

- Its use and importance

Books which are special to Christian people

- The Bible
- Hymn, song and prayer books
- Palestine (map) in biblical times
- The Bible in worship

SACRED BOOKS

Judaism

- Looking at the Ten Commandments
- The Talmud and the Torah

The *Ramayana*, *Mahabharata* and the *Bhavagad Gita*

- The *Ramayana* – Rama and Sita
- The children's *Mahabharata*

The Qu'ran

- Its appearance, handling and use

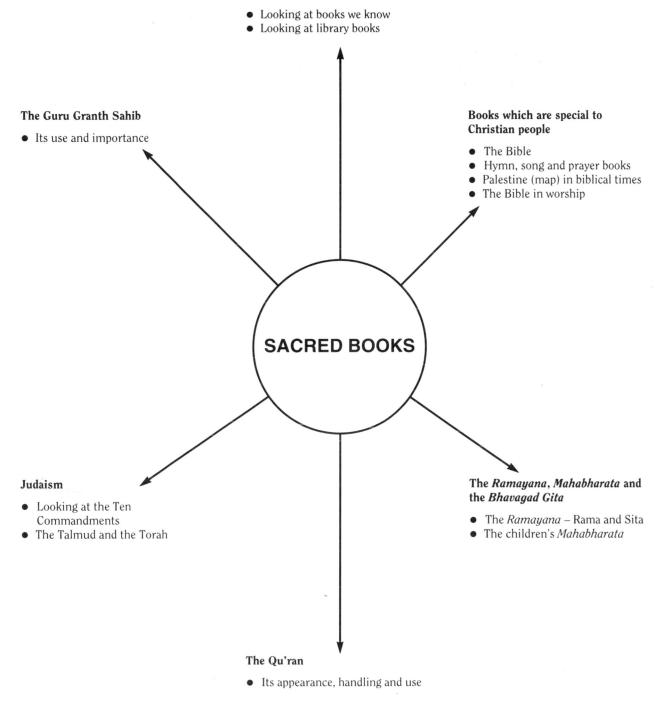

LEARNING OBJECTIVES

- To be aware of books important to us and books which are precious to religious communities.
- To explore ways in which sacred books are regarded by believers both in the home and in places of worship.
- To become familiar with stories and short extracts from such sacred books as the Bible, the Qur'an, the children's *Mahabharata*, the Torah and the Guru Granth Sahib.

STARTING POINTS

Cvi

- Make a list on the blackboard of people the children know in their local community who they have faith in to give help and support: for example, the family doctor or vet. The children can draw pictures of these people, writing their titles underneath and what they do.

- Ask the children how many of them know a religious person in the community who helps others through his or her work. Can they think of different ways in which others in the community rely on this person to give help, both inside and outside the place of worship?

- Collect pictures or copies of sacred books that people with faith use. Pupils can think of describing words for the appearance of the books. Write down the names of these books on cards and place the cards by

each book to make a display, and to enable the children to become familiar with the names. Explain to the children that they are all going to hear stories from these books about people with faith and what happened to them in their lives through having faith in their God.

- List the names of Jesus, Muhammad, Buddha, Krishna, Moses and Guru Nanak and say the name of the faith each represents. Devise a simple game based on their existing knowledge. Divide the class into teams and as the gamemaster (either the teacher or a selected pupil) gives a name or faith, children can shout out a corresponding word associated with it (for example, Hinduism/Krishna; Islam/mosque; Moses/Egypt; Jesus/Christians, etc.) and collect points.

- Learn and sing together the topic song, **Sacred books**.

Area of study 1

HOW BOOKS ARE IMPORTANT TO US

C51 –52

Purpose

To be aware of books important to us and books which are precious to religious communities; to explore ways in which sacred books are regarded by believers both at home and at places of worship.

Activity 1: Looking at books we know

[A] Arrange with parents for children to bring a favourite book to school. Divide the class into pairs and ask the children to show their book to their partner and share with them the reasons why they like it. Children should listen carefully to the points made by their partners. Ask each child to give one reason why their partner likes the book they have selected and to hold it up for everyone to see. Invite further comments from the children about their own books and emphasise the fact that some books are special to us and that we often like to read them over and over again.

[B] Use **Copymaster 51** (My favourite book). The children can draw a picture of the front cover, write in the author's name and say underneath why they like it.

Activity 2: Looking at library books

[A] Liaise with the Junior Department for the children to visit the library or visit the local library if the

Education Department there invites the children for storytelling sessions. Allow the children to examine the books carefully and to find out how they are made. With the help of the librarian look at the way in which the children's books are organised: story, information, picture books, adventure books, and so on.

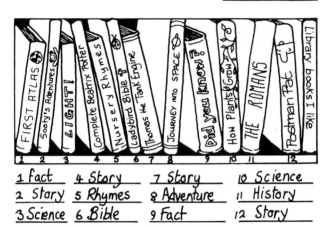

✓ Use **Copymaster 52** (Library books I like) to fill in the blank spines with titles discovered in the library that they particularly liked or found interesting. Ensure different sections are covered – for example, a picture book, an adventure book, an information book, a science book, etc. Underneath the books they fill in the type of book corresponding to the number given on the library the shelf.

1 Fact	4 Story	7 Story	10 Science
2 Story	5 Rhymes	8 Adventure	11 History
3 Science	6 Bible	9 Fact	12 Story

B Divide the class into small groups with an able reader in charge. Give each group a large sheet of paper and make lists of the different kinds of books in the children's section, writing them in alphabetical order.

Area of study 2	# BOOKS WHICH ARE SPECIAL TO CHRISTIAN PEOPLE	C53 –57 ▶

Purpose
To examine books which are special to people with faith.

Activity 1: Looking at the Bible

A Tell the children that just as they have books which are precious to them, so do members of religious communities, people who believe in God. Point out that like the letter children take home from school in a communication from the Headteacher which helps the school community to run smoothly, the message from God in the holy books helps members of religious communities to live their lives positively.

B Give the children flashcards on which the word 'Bible' is printed with a picture of the Bible underneath it. Then give out flashcards on which are written '66 books', 'Old Testament' and 'New Testament'. Explain to the children that there are 66 books written over hundreds of years telling us about God's work among the Jews (the Old Testament) as well as stories of Jesus' life and work and what happened afterwards (New Testament). Tell the children that the Old Testament is used by three religions, Judaism, Islam and Christianity, because all three faiths share the same stories about famous leaders of the past, such as Abraham and Moses. (Flashcards on which are written the words, 'Jews', 'Muslims' and 'Christians' can also be distributed.)

C Write down the words 'New Testament' and 'gospel', explaining that 'gospel' means 'good news' about Jesus, and writing the names of the four gospel writers underneath. Take each gospel writer in turn, reading the accounts given in **Matthew, Mark, Luke and John** (p. 70) so that children will be aware of who gave us much of the information we have about Jesus. Invite pupils to write or draw one detail or fact about the evangelists in the appropriate place on the sheet of paper until you have filled each column.

D Give out **Copymaster 53** (My Bible library card). The children should fill in the information in the spaces in the three sections, cut out the copymaster and fold the two outer sections, 'Bible contents' and 'The New Testament' inwards. When folded, they can design a front cover for their Bible information leaflet and name it. Show the class Programme Two, 'A Surprise Death', of the series *Coming Together*, part of which shows how children made a model of the Bible as a library.

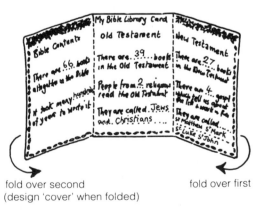

fold over second
(design 'cover' when folded)   fold over first

E Use **Copymaster 54** (The four gospel writers) to consolidate work on the New Testament. The children can colour in the pictures of the gospel writers and fill in the blanks in the sentences underneath the pictures using the correct word from those at the bottom of the copymaster.

F Tell the children that the Bible is widely read throughout the world today. It can be found in all kinds of places in the community. Can pupils give any examples? Six buildings where a Bible is commonly found appear on **Copymaster 55** (Our community Bible): ask children to identify these, writing the correct name under each picture which can be coloured in.

Activity 2: Looking at hymn, song and prayer books

A Examine school hymn, song and prayer books as well as Church of England ones and look together at some of the prayers for special occasions such as Christmas, Easter, infant baptism and weddings.

✓ Choose a prayer often used in assembly and write this on the board. The children should be practised now at expressing themselves in prayer form (see **Food**, p. 34 and **Worship**, p. 40): encourage them to compile some brief, personal prayers and write them on the prayer book pages on **Copymaster 56** (My prayers). Advise them that these prayers are for their own private use. They can stick the copymaster into their personal workbooks and refer to the prayers at certain times during the day (before assembly or meals may be especially suitable).

B Return to the hymn and song books. Ask pupils to tell you why they think music is such an important part of worship. So they enjoy singing a song? Do they think it is a good way of expressing our feelings to God? Write the word 'hymn' on the board and tell them that this is a special type of song – one which is dedicated to God during worship.

C Revise the topic song, **Sacred books**, or attempt to compose and perform simple hymns using homemade instruments (shakers, milk bottles, etc.).

Activity 3: Looking at Palestine in biblical times

A Study a map of Palestine in biblical times and show the children drawings of the kind of homes in which people, and Jesus in particular, may have lived (cross-reference **Birth Celebrations**, p. 20). Consider the methods of construction of the houses and discuss the types of material which might have been available (stone, mud, brick); consider also the climate in Palestine and the clothes worn both 1 000 years ago and today.

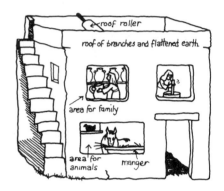

B Sit with the children and read the short story **Daniel and Miriam** (p. 71), discussing it with them afterwards. The children can make up a story about Miriam's and Daniel's visits to Aunty Ruth and Uncle Ben.

C Show the children slides of Bedouin tents and flat-roofed houses. Create together a model of a Palestinian house using card, crayons and a small amount of flattened straw for the roof.

Activity 4: The Bible in worship

A Recall the children's visit to their local church (see **Worship**, p. 40) and draw their attention to the

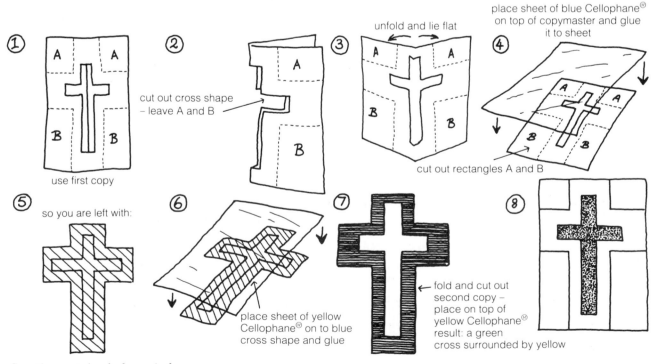

Creating a stained-glass window

building's windows. Can they remember what was special about them? Hold up some photographs of stained-glass windows and notice with the children their themes and symbols from the Bible.

 The children can create a stained-glass window which shows the Christian symbol of the cross. Point out that all Bibles show a cross, many on the front cover and always on the inside of the book.

Make two copies of **Copymaster 57** (Stained-glass window) and ask pupils to fold both copies outwards along the two lines running down and across the central cross shape. Then put one copymaster to one side, and using the other, place a blue sheet of cellophane on it,

cut to the size of the copymaster, and glue it to the sheet. Cut out the two squares (A) and two rectangles (B). Lie a yellow piece of cellophane on top of the cross (copymaster size like the blue one) and glue to secure. Place one other copy of Copymaster 57 (cut out) on top of the yellow Cellophane®. You should now have a green cross surrounded by yellow! (See p. 66.)

C Read the story of **Mary Jones and her Bible** (p. 71), then give out **Copymaster 58** (Mary Jones and her Bible) which shows illustrations of Mary Jones to colour in and the story of how she obtained her own copy of the Bible. Pupils can cut out each section and mount them on to card to make a booklet with an attractive cover.

THE RAMAYANA, MAHABHARATA AND THE BHAVAGAD GITA

Area of study 3

Purpose
To familiarise the children with Indian devotional literature.

Activity 1: Sacred books of India
A Make the classroom atmosphere as Indian as possible with posters, incense sticks and lanterns. Ask children what they can remember about Hindu gods and goddesses (see **Worship**, p. 42) and write a list of their responses on the board.

B Show the children the *Ramayana* and point out Rama and Sita on the posters you have gathered.

C Tell the story **Rama and Sita** to the class (p. 71). Alternatively, this story can be recorded before the lesson with appropriate Indian music also included at the beginning and end as well as at certain points within it. Shadow puppets can be used to develop the story. Explain to the children that the god Rama is thought of in a special way in that he returned to earth as Lord Vishnu to rid it from the evil monster, Ravana.

D Make lanterns and masks and ask the children to draw, colour and cut out the characters in the Rama and Sita story.

Activity 2: Introducing the *Mahabharata* and *Bhavagad Gita*
A The children's *Mahabharata* can be introduced in a similar way to the *Ramayana* in that it has a wide variety of stories based around the two families, the Pandavas and the Kauravas, in which there are living battles for supremacy, again of good over evil.

B Explain to the children that Krishna, believed to be Lord Vishnu returning in another form, is considered to be God by many Hindus and his 'Bhavagad Gita' or 'Song to the Lord' is contained within the *Mahabharata* and is an important source of Hindu worship.

C Invite Hindu visitors to show pictures of home shrines and help the children to construct a shrine in the classroom. Encourage pupils to ask their visitors questions concerning Hindu sacred books and how they are used in worship.

THE QUR'AN

Area of study 4

 C58

Purpose
To look at the importance of the Qur'an to people of the Muslim faith.

Activity: Looking at the Qur'an
A Make a paper word tree, on which the words 'Muslim', 'Islam', 'Sura', 'Allah' and 'Qur'an' are clearly marked.

B Present a copy of the Qur'an on its stand and explain that this is the most holy book of the faith known as Islam. Show 'A Hindu Way of Life', Programme Seven of *Coming Together* which also tells the story of Muhammad's experience when the Angel Gabriel related the first verse or Sura of the Qur'an.

C Tell the children about Muhammad's wife, Khadijah, a rich business woman who loved and supported him very much.

D Convey to the children the reverence with which the Qur'an is treated. Mention that it should be wrapped in a cloth and, if handled, must have clean paper put around it. Put the words 'A recitation' beside 'Qur'an' on the word tree and explain that Muslims recite passages from the Qur'an when they worship and pray.

E Visit a local mosque school where Muslim children learn Arabic so that they will be able to read and recite the Qur'an. The children may be able to hear some of the songs which are sung to help students learn the duties of a Muslim. If a visit is not possible, invite the imam to the class so that he can explain the purpose of a mosque school and show children some of the materials used to teach the Qur'an to students.

F Inform the class that the Qur'an has 114 chapters and that these teach Muslims about how to live their lives and talks about marriage, war, work and property in particular.

G Write the Arabic word for the Prophet Muhammad on the blackboard. Give pupils **Copymaster 59** (Muhammad) which shows the Arabic within a decorative border. Ask them to fill in the lettering with black felt-tip pen so that they become accustomed to the appearance and style of Arabic writing. The geometrical border can be decorated in bright colours and the copymaster displayed.

H Read the short story of Nawab **Reading from the Qur'an** (p. 72) to the children which gives an example of how a young boy went about reading from the Qur'an in a school assembly.

| Area of study 5 | **JUDAISM** | C60 |

Purpose
To re-examine the Ten Commandments, and to look at the importance of the Bible, Talmud and Torah to Jewish people.

Activity 1: Revising the Ten Commandments and introducing the Talmud
A Sit the children around a table on which there is one copy of the Bible, one of the Talmud and posters showing Jews at worship in the synagogue and processing with the scrolls.

B Remind the children of the stories they already know about Moses (see pp. 24, 48) and retell the giving of the Ten Commandments on Mount Sinai. After a suitable pause, ask pupils to write down as many of the Commandments as they can remember. When they have finished, ask them to look at their completed Copymaster 38 (see **Worship**, p. 44) and compare their list filling in any omissions.

C Tell the children that when Moses had rescued the Israelites from Pharaoh, the Egyptian King, he took them into the desert to escape. Ask the children to imagine thousands of people all with their families, their animals and belongings moving together. Show them recently recorded news clips of refugees on the move. How do they think these people must feel?

D Sit with the class at a table again on which you have placed copies of the Bible and the Talmud. Inform the children that the Scriptures play a vital part in Jewish life and worship. Show them the Talmud again. Explain its importance to Jewish law and read stories of the early rabbis to the class. Add the Talmud to the book corner in the classroom.

Activity 2: Looking at the Torah
A Show the children two small scrolls, beautifully covered, and explain with the use of slides and photographs that the most important part of the Scriptures is the Torah, the first five books of the Old Testament: can they tell you what these are (cross-reference **Worship**, p. 45). Write the names of the books on the blackboard or a flipchart.

B Write the word 'Torah' and its meaning, 'Teaching', on a large card for the children to copy and decorate. Add the word 'Shema' and write this on the board for the children to read and learn: 'Hear, O Israel, the Lord our God is one Lord and you shall love the Lord your God with all your soul and with all your might'.

C Remind pupils of their visit to a synagogue (see **Worship**, p. 45) and recap on the positions of the ark and the *bimah*. Tell them that there is a festival called Simcha Torah, the 'Rejoicing of the Law'.

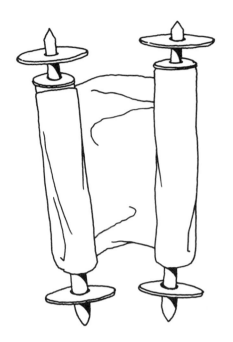

two tightly rolled pieces
of card with pointed
paper ends

glue circles to
rolled card

long rectangular
piece of paper,
dampened and left to dry
(to resemble parchment)

two kitchen towel rolls

eight cardboard
circles to be positioned
as shown

D Watch Programme Six, 'Judaism', of *Coming Together* to see the procession of the Torah around the synagogue when it has been taken from the ark. Look at the purpose of the *yad* with the children, the finger or hand-shaped pointer which avoids the touching of the Torah by dirty hands.

E Show the children some pictures of important objects seen in a synagogue in the order shown on **Copymaster 60** (Synagogue I-spy). The children can colour the pictures in and attempt to label them.

F Read the story **The tattooed Torah** by Marvell Ginsherg retold by Monica Price (p. 72). Let the children draw and paint the tattered Torah in his purple velvet cover and silver bells. They can then write a paragraph following on from the story of the tattered Torah in which the little Torah tells the other Torahs how he felt during the procession.

G Make scrolls with the class and write biblical stories of Moses, Abraham, Jacob and Joseph carefully on them.

Area of study 6

THE GURU GRANTH SAHIB ➤

Purpose
To study the Guru Granth Sahib and its importance to people of the Sikh faith.

Activity: Looking at the Guru Granth Sahib
A Watch Programme Four, 'Symbols of Faith and Justice', the Sikh programme of *Coming Together*, filmed in a gurdwara, then show the children pictures and posters of the Guru Granth Sahib which have been taken in temples and home shrines.

B If possible, take the children to a home shrine of kindly Sikhs in the local community. Observe carefully the requirements to remove shoes and cover heads.

Note Wherever the Guru Granth Sahib is found, that home, hotel, school, etc., becomes a gurdwara during the time the Guru Granth Sahib is there. Heads must be covered, shoes removed and before that a bath must be taken by all present. Therefore, it is easier to take the children to a home shrine to see the Guru Granth Sahib than it is for the Sikh holy book to be brought to school.

Ask the granthi (reader) or temple elder if he or she would be willing to sit behind the Guru Granth Sahib and wave the *chauri* to show the children how it is used.

If possible, children could see the bedroom where the Guru Granth Sahib is laid to rest at night and where it is awakened and taken into procession every morning. Point out the beautiful cover which the holy book will be wearing. Tell pupils that the book is regarded as a person, a guru in its own right, and gives advice to Sikhs in all situations.

The Guru Granth Sahib at a home shrine

69

C After the trip to the home shrine, a Sikh mother may be willing to visit the class to speak with the children about the importance to family life of the Guru Granth Sahib.

D Tell the class that there were ten gurus in the Sikh religion. Show them paintings of Guru Nanak and of Guru Gobind Singh. Briefly describe the meeting the latter had with his Sikhs when he announced there would be no more human gurus after him and that the Guru Granth Sahib had the power of the living Guru for ever.

E Remind children of the slides and pictures they have seen of the Golden Temple at Amritsar (see **Worship**, p. 42). Read them the story **The temple at Amritsar** (p. 72) which tells of how the Golden Temple came to be built and the first Guru Granth Sahib placed within it.

F Explain to the children that a religious ceremony cannot take place unless the Guru Granth Sahib is present. Sikh people who cannot afford a copy of the holy book borrow it for special occasions such as weddings.

Show the children selections from a Sikh wedding ceremony video and look at ways that the Guru Granth Sahib is used with them.

G Show the children the *Japji* (Sikh morning prayers). Explain that these and other sacred books were written by Guru Gobind Singh. Place them reverently in the book corner together with photographs of a Guru Granth Sahib or books of Sikh prayers for the children to look at.

TOPIC STORIES ▶

Matthew, Mark, Luke and John

Matthew

Matthew collected money from people's wages which had to be paid to the Roman government. The Romans ruled Palestine 2 000 years ago when Jesus was on the earth.

No one liked Matthew because he took more money from the people than he should have done and kept it for himself. He was a tax collector and was unkind to the people.

One day Jesus went to the market place and walked up to a table where Matthew was sitting with a big scroll which had a lot of names on it. Jesus did not give his name and Matthew looked up at him. He thought Jesus had come to pay his taxes.

'Well, who are you?' asked Matthew at last.

Jesus looked steadily at Matthew. 'Follow me,' he said.

Matthew stared at the stranger. He knew he must go with him. He left his table and called to someone else to take over.

He became a disciple of Jesus and because he had cheated people out of money, he gave twice that amount of money to the poor people of the area. Later, he wrote a book about Jesus.

Mark

Mark was a teenager and he lived in Jerusalem. His mother had a big house with a large room upstairs which people rented from her on festival days to have special meals with their friends.

Mark was a Jew and on the day when all Jews would be having their Passover meals, Mark's mother sent him to the city gate to meet two men.

'Carry a jug of water on your head,' she told him.

'That's girls' work,' objected Mark at once for only girls went to the wells for water.

'Yes, I know,' answered his mother. 'This is why I want you to do it because you will be noticed by the two men. Bring them here to me, but don't talk to them. Make sure they see you and follow you.'

Mark did as his mother asked and as soon as he reached the gates of Jerusalem he saw two men, one tall, one shorter, talking to one another. They noticed him, but said nothing. Mark led them back to his mother's house and then helped them to prepare the room upstairs for the Passover meal. Later, more men came, twelve altogether and Jesus. Mark had seen Jesus in the city and admired him.

Jesus was arrested that night. After he and his friends had eaten the Passover meal they went to the Mount of Olives to a small garden where Jesus prayed to God. Soon after they left the house the soldiers came to look for Jesus, but left to make their way to the garden when they found he had gone. Mark went after the soldiers because he hoped he could reach Jesus before the soldiers and warn him. He was too late. By the time he got there, Jesus had been arrested. One of the soldiers ran after Mark but the boy escaped.

Many years later, Mark became a friend of Peter, Jesus' best-known follower. Peter told Mark the whole story of Jesus' life and work and Mark wrote it all down.

Luke

Luke was a Greek doctor and he didn't believe in God at all because he didn't like the way in which people became ill and suffered. He never met Jesus but one day he was called to the home of a sick man called Paul who was the first Christian missionary. Luke and Paul became good friends and Luke travelled with Paul for many years.

70

Later, Luke made up his mind to write the true story of Jesus and his work and he travelled everywhere that Jesus had gone. He interviewed hundreds of people, among them Jesus' mother, Mary.

There are two books written by Luke, the Gospel of Luke and another one called the Acts of the Apostles, which follows all that Jesus' disciples did after Jesus had left them and gone to Heaven.

John

John was the youngest of the disciples and he was Jesus' special friend. John had a brother, James, and the two young men were fishermen. They left their jobs to follow Jesus.

John was one of Jesus' special group of disciples – Peter, James and John – who went everywhere with Jesus.

Thereafter, John's book tells of everything Jesus did and gives more of his special teachings.

Daniel and Miriam

Daniel and Miriam loved to spend their summer holidays in Jerusalem with Aunty Ruth and Uncle Ben. When it was too hot to sleep indoors at night, the children would be allowed to climb the stairs to the flat roof of their Aunty and Uncle's house and sleep there. They liked to look up at the starry sky and make up stories about the moon and the stars.

Sometimes Uncle Ben took them into the countryside and this was even more exciting because they would all sleep in a big tent.

Sometimes they even went into the desert with Uncle Ben when he went on business trips. They would see the black tents of the Bedouin tribes and when they arrived home, they would tell Aunty Ruth all about their journey and draw pictures of the tents for her.

Mary Jones and her Bible

Mary Jones was a little Welsh girl who wanted a Bible of her own very much. Mary and her parents were very poor but they were happy and every week they went to the little village church to hear the stories of Jesus and of the prophets read from the Bible by the vicar.

'I'd love to be able to have my own Bible,' sighed Mary, but Bibles were expensive and her parents could not afford to buy her one.

'When you learn to read, you can come to my house and read my Bible,' said a kind lady who had her own copy of the Bible.

Mary started school soon afterwards and worked so hard at her reading that she was soon able to go to the kind lady's house and read verses from the Bible. How proud and pleased she was and so were her parents.

Mary began to run errands after school and do all kinds of odd jobs for people so that she could save up for her Bible. At last she had enough money but there were no Bibles to be had in the village and the nearest town was 25 miles away. Imagine walking 25 miles in all kinds of weather. Mary managed it but when she arrived at a shop which sold Bibles, she found that there were only three left and these had all been promised to people who had been saving up for Bibles like herself.

The shopkeeper could see how disappointed Mary was and he could not believe that such a little girl had walked 25 miles. He went into the back of his shop and brought out his own Bible which he gave to Mary. He made her rest in his shop for a while and walked with her some of the way home.

This man was so surprised at Mary's action that he founded a special society which he called The British and Foreign Bible Society. In future, there would be plenty of Bibles to go round so that everyone, rich or poor, would be able to buy one as cheaply as possible.

Rama and Sita

In the city of Ayodyha there was once a King called Dasaratha who had three wives and four sons. Prince Rama was the eldest, a specially gifted young man who was married to a beautiful princess called Sita.

King Dasaratha decided to retire and make Rama King in his place. But his second wife, the mother of Bharata, the King's son, had once saved King Dasaratha's life. In return for this, she insisted that the son, Bharata, should be King and that Prince Rama be banished to the forest. Prince Rama agreed to the banishment. Bharata was made King and Rama, Sita and Lakshmana, one of the other princes, left the palace dressed as hermits.

Ravana, King of the Monsters wanted to destroy Rama and Sita and there were many battles between the princes and the demon king. One day, Ravana took the shape of a deer and led Rama into the forest. Once he had caused Rama to lose his way, Ravana took on the shape of a hermit and went to the house in the forest where Sita was waiting for Rama to return. Ravana knocked at the door and persuaded the kind-hearted Sita that he was a poor hermit desperately needing food. Sita let him in and Ravana at once became the monster again with ten heads and twenty arms. He carried Sita off to his kingdom in Sri Lanka. When Rama and his brother, Lakshmana returned, they found Sita had gone and eventually they discovered that Ravana had taken her away to the island of Sri Lanka.

It was Hanuman, the Monkey King who saved Sita from the demon king. There was a channel of water between India and Sri Lanka which it was difficult to cross. Hanuman leapt across the water, found Ravana's kingdom and Princess Sita and said he would bring Rama to rescue her. Ravana set Hanuman's tail on fire but Hanuman burnt down Ravana's city with his tail. He and his monkeys formed a bridge across the channel to Sri Lanka so that Rama could cross, kill Ravana and rescue Sita.

Rama and Sita's return as King and Queen of Ayodhya is celebrated at the Diwali festival. Hundreds of Diwali lamps are lit all over India and in Hindu homes here to welcome back Rama and Sita as well as to allow Lakshmi, goddess of good fortune into each home.

The full story of Rama and Sita's banishment is told in the book, The Ramayana.

Reading from the Qu'ran

Nawab was asked to read some verses from the Holy Qu'ran during school assembly. He agreed to do so but first he had to go to the cloakroom and wash his hands because he was not allowed to touch the Qu'ran with unwashed hands.

When he had washed himself Nawab took his copy of the Qu'ran from a beautiful box with an embroidered cover. Nawab touched the Qu'ran with his head and kissed the cover before placing it on a stand and beginning to read.

All except one chapter has the same beginning and Nawab read, 'In the name of Allah, the compassionate, the Merciful' before continuing the chapter.

The tattooed Torah

The little Torah lived in a synagogue with other larger Torahs in Czechoslovakia before the war of 1939–45. He was dressed in a purple velvet cloak and his real purpose was to be carried around the synagogue on Sabbath mornings and holy days. All the Torahs were embroidered with silver bells which made soft tinkling sounds as they were taken from the ark.

The little Torah loved processions. Children would hold him gently and carefully and he felt important even though he was the smallest Torah.

Then Czechoslovakia was invaded and men burst into the synagogue, tore open the ark and stole the beautiful cloaks and silver bells. All the Torahs were thrown into a dirty truck and then into an old warehouse.

Someone prodded the little Torah with a stick and injured him. He cried bitterly but no one heard him. The Torahs all stayed in the warehouse until long after the war was over because everyone forgot about them.

A Jewish school in America sent Mr Weil, a member of their congregation, to Prague to see if he could find a small Torah for the children to carry during synagogue services. Mr Weil had heard that there were 1 500 Torahs in the warehouse and that few people knew about them. When Mr Weil found the warehouse and saw the injured and torn Torahs he was deeply upset. He cried and cried, the tears rolling down his cheeks.

Before returning to America Mr Weil went to London and spoke to the Jews in Westminster. He told the congregation about the Torahs and they were sad too.
'We must find the money to save the Torahs and bring them to new homes,' they said and he was given the job of making sure that all the Torahs were flown to London for cleaning and repair. Soon they would all be dressed in velvet coverings with silver bells again.

As soon as Mr Weil saw the tattered little Torah he knew that this was the scroll he had been looking for.
'How would you like to come to America with me and be loved and cared for there?' Mr Weil asked Little Torah.
Little Torah was overjoyed. He went to London with the biggest Torahs, was cleaned and repaired and then went to America where Mr and Mrs Weil and many other willing people made beautiful velvet mantles for him and dressed him in gold and silver bells.

What a proud little Torah he was that first Sabbath morning when he was taken from the ark for the first time. The children had been told he was there and they could not wait to see him and carry him lovingly in procession around the synagogue. The little Torah was happier than he had ever been in his life.

The temple at Amritsar

The Emperor Akbar was a supporter and friend of the Sikh faith and he often visited the third Guru, Amar Das, at his headquarters. Guru Amar Das made the Emperor do the same as all the other visitors – share a meal in the Sikh kitchen with everyone else before meeting the Guru.

Emperor Akbar wanted to give Guru Amar Das a present of some land but the Guru refused to accept it. He did not like to be given presents. The Emperor gave the land to Bhani Das, the Guru's daughter, instead of the Guru and Amar Das had to agree to that.

Bhani Das married Ram Das who became the fourth Sikh Guru. Ram Das built the city of Amritsar, the Sikh holy city on the land that the Emperor had given to his wife and he created a pool in which the most beautiful temple he could imagine would be situated.

The Golden Temple at Amritsar was finished by Ram Das and Bhani Das' son, Arjan, the fifth Guru. Each Guru had kept the sacred hymns of the previous one and to these Guru Arjan added the writings of Muslims and Hindus whose ideas were similar to those of the Sikhs.

In April, 1604, the first Guru Granth Sahib was placed in the Golden Temple of Amritsar. A special ceremony was held and visitors came from all over the world.

The tenth Guru, Gobind Singh rewrote the entire Guru Granth Sahib from memory after it had been lost. The book in the Golden Temple was known as 'Adi Granth' (original book).

Beginnings

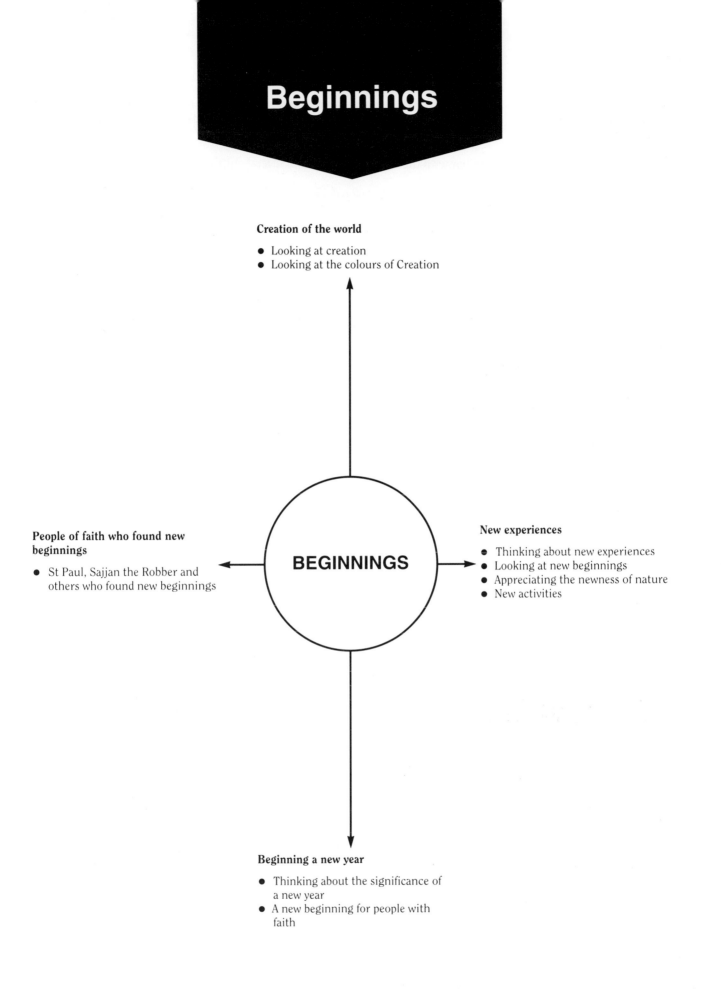

Creation of the world

- Looking at creation
- Looking at the colours of Creation

People of faith who found new beginnings

- St Paul, Sajjan the Robber and others who found new beginnings

BEGINNINGS

New experiences

- Thinking about new experiences
- Looking at new beginnings
- Appreciating the newness of nature
- New activities

Beginning a new year

- Thinking about the significance of a new year
- A new beginning for people with faith

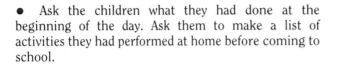

LEARNING OBJECTIVES

- To help children to become familiar with the creation stories from several cultures and to offer their own ideas on how the world began.
- To encourage children to look at their own personal beginnings and to consider stories connected with themselves and others.
- To present customs connected with new year ceremonies and the bearing these have on new opportunities.
- To consider how belief has changed the lives of two people who became the first missionaries in the religions of Christianity and Sikhism.

STARTING POINTS
Cvii

- Ask the children what they had done at the beginning of the day. Ask them to make a list of activities they had performed at home before coming to school.

- Give pupils a sheet of paper divided into squares big enough to draw small pictures in. Ask them to do a comic strip story showing what they had done after waking up that day, such as washing, dressing, eating breakfast, putting on their coat, and so on. Look at the pictures together and talk about them.

- Ask the children if they had looked out of their bedroom or lounge window that morning. What had they noticed? Did they see anything they liked in the world outside? Was it light? What could they hear: the traffic, the postman, the birds? Was the sun shining or was it raining?

- Introduce the idea that many people believe God created the world all around us, the world in which they woke up that morning. Explain to them that they are going to hear all about creation.

- Read the words of the song 'Wonderful World' (Louis Armstrong) or the hymn 'Morning has Broken' and talk about the things in our world that are mentioned. If possible, play the recordings. Alternatively, read the children a general poem about the world around us. Ask them to draw or paint pictures of their idea of a wonderful world.

- Teach the topic song, **In the beginning**. Children can also write their own songs and perform them in groups to the rest of the class.

CREATION OF THE WORLD
Area of study 1

C61 –63

Purpose
To introduce creation stories of several faiths to the children.

Activity 1: How did the world begin?
A   Sit with the children around a large globe. Help them to locate where their country, city or town is and inform them that the earth is like a huge ball which rotates through a full circle once every 24 hours. Let the children draw round circular templates to show earth by night and by day with the sun beaming light upon it. Ask them to write 'light' and 'dark' against each side of their drawing, colouring the dark side blue and the light side light blue and green.

B   Watch a video or slides of a sunrise accompanying it with appropriate music or a tape recording of the dawn chorus just before the sun rises. Then read **The creation story from Genesis** (p. 79) and prepare a dance/drama with the children showing the seven days

of creation or make a wall frieze showing everything that God created according to the Genesis story.

C   Use **Copymaster 61** (The seven days of creation) to show all that happened in sequence. The children can cut out the pictures and labels and mount them on to a single sheet of stiff paper to make a 'creation fan'; they will need help to gather and secure the paper at the bottom. (See p. 75.)

D   Read the two creation stories, **The Hindu creation story** (p. 79) and **Woman Fallen from the Sky** (a North American Indian myth, p. 79) to the children, then divide the class into groups. Put the names of the three creation stories they have learnt about on the board and take each one in turn asking the children to tell the story to the person sitting next to them. Let the children choose either the Hindu or North American Indian creation story and make a booklet with drawings and short sentences.

stick pictures and labels on to paper

Night, day   Water, heaven   Seas, earth

Making a creation fan

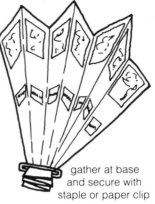

fold

gather at base
and secure with
staple or paper clip

E Talk to the children about their own ideas concerning how the world began. Remind them that their ideas of how the world began are as important and valid as the ones they have just learnt. Encourage them to paint pictures, write descriptions or organise their thoughts into a story sequence or 'cartoon strip'.

Activity 2: The colours of creation

A Ask the school caretaker to attach a hose to an outside tap and to stand with his back to the sun in the playground so that the children can see the rainbow colours in the water.

Explain how light bends as it goes through water and that each colour of light bends by a different amount so it can be seen separately. Tell them the bands of coloured light make a rainbow. Show pupils a large picture of a rainbow and identify the colours.

B Tell the children that the rainbow once meant a new beginning for the world and read them the story **Noah and the rainbow** (p. 80).

Collect with the children as many pictures of animals, birds and reptiles as possible. These can be copied or stuck on to card, cut out and mounted all the way around the classroom to make a winding wall frieze entitled , 'Noah and the rainbow'. A toy ark can be borrowed and placed in a corner to mark the end of the procession.

Listen to the music called *Captain Noah and his Floating Zoo* with the children. Point to their work on the wall as the music progresses. They can sing to the tape and learn the 'Rain' chorus in song 1, the arrival of the flood in song 5 and the contrasting sight of the rainbow in song 10.

C Use **Copymaster 62** (Animal pairs) to pair off the examples of animals, birds and reptiles to be taken into Noah's ark. Then let the children act out any part of the story and make up a special 'rainbow dance'.

Children will enjoy creating a 'Noah and the rainbow' *wall frieze for your classroom*

D **Copymaster 63** (Rainbow colours) provides a rainbow grid to work on. Children should examine the separate colours of the rainbow and create their own rainbow, marking the colours in the correct order.

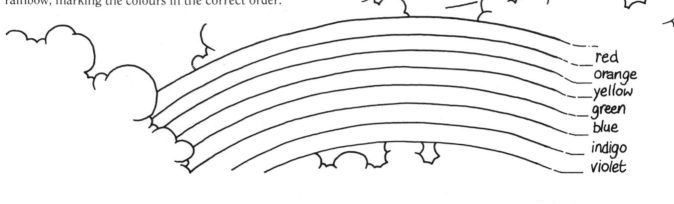

red
orange
yellow
green
blue
indigo
violet

Area of study 2

NEW EXPERIENCES

C64 –69

Purpose
To focus on feelings which children have experienced so far.

Activity 1: Thinking about new experiences.
A Use **Copymaster 64** (My beginnings) to look with the class at the beginnings common to everyone – a new baby, the baby in the pram (sitting up), the baby starting to walk, sitting in a high chair eating by themselves, the toddler, and the first day at school. The children can colour in the pictures and number them in the right order.

B Discuss with the children how they were feeling on their first day and school and give suggestions:

● Betty thought her Mum stood in the entry by the school for the whole of the day. Whenever she felt upset she'd think, 'Mummy is standing outside. I'll be alright.'
● Ben didn't want to go to school at all. He clung to his mother and cried and his mother asked the teacher, 'Shall I take him home and try again tomorrow?'
   'No,' said the teacher, firmly. 'Bill and John will look after Ben.'
   When the two boys came over to him, Ben shouted, 'Go away! I want to go home.'

'I was like that, too,' John told him. 'Come over here and try out the pedal car. It's really great.'
   Ben left his mother and followed the two boys.

Ask the children if it helps to have other children make special efforts to be friendly like John did with Ben.

✓ Use **Copymaster 65** (My first day at school) for the children to draw their own pictures of others they were with on their first day at school. While they are drawing their pictures talk to the children about the fact that their first day at school is not just a new beginning for them but for other people around them like those they are drawing in their pictures. They can then write down a few words or phrases in the lower half of the copymaster to record how they felt and what they remembered they did at this very important time.

Activity 2: New beginnings
A Remind the children of their pictorial diaries containing photographs of themselves as babies (see **Birth celebrations**, p. 16).

B Use **Copymaster 66** (Growing skills) to draw a picture in each box of something they could do for each year of their lives so far, putting in the last box something they have just learnt to do. Give them the following descriptions to help them to get started:

● Mary could reach the top of the kitchen table when she was three. She didn't need to be lifted up any more. Her Grandad told her she was clever and gave her some sweets.
● Martin wanted a scooter for his sixth birthday but Mum said he wasn't tall enough and would have to wait until Christmas. Every day, Martin asked his mother to measure him against the wall and at last his Mum said, 'Yes, alright. I'll ask Father Christmas to bring your scooter.'

C Look with the children at such beginnings as going to the shop and going to school by oneself for the first time. Give them special folders marked 'Beginnings' so that they may enter in these anything new they experience such as learning to swim, riding a bike, playing rounders or football, taking the dog out by oneself, accepting responsibility for a younger child or for a family pet, going away on holiday.

D Ask the children to write or draw in their diaries anything they were not happy about at the end of the previous week and how weekends are always new and different. Now use **Copymaster 67** (A new week) to decide what they would like to happen at home and at school *this* week (getting on with brothers and sisters, doing special jobs at home, getting on well in class and at playtime).

Activity 3: Appreciating the newness of nature

A Take the children to the local park. Look at seasonal flowers, trees and plants. Ask one of the gardeners to explain to the children how far in advance he must plant seeds for each season and for special displays. Tell the children the story of **Johnny's field** (p. 80) as they are standing together in the park.

B In the classroom, give the children tissue paper and paints. Let them draw and paint the flowers and trees they saw in the park. Alternatively, obtain a variety of bulbs: plant these and watch them grow with the children.

C Use **Copymaster 68** (Flowers and seasons) to find out which flowers have new beginnings at certain seasons of the year, matching the flower picture with its season by drawing a linking line on the sheet.

Activity 4: New activities and hobbies

A Sit informally with the children and look at the activities they have chosen to begin such as Rainbow Guides and Beaver Scouts, joining a choir or club, taking up special hobbies.

B Write the word 'hobby' on the board. Can the children tell you what this means? Explain that it is important to develop interests or hobbies with our families, friends or on our own which allow us to participate in fulfilling activities. Give examples such as swimming, bike riding, reading, Scouts, etc.

✓ Make a list of some of the activities in which the children are involved and use **Copymaster 69** (What do I do after school?) to tick some off these activities and colour in the pictures. The last two boxes have been left blank for the children to think of other activities with which they may be involved.

BEGINNING A NEW YEAR

Purpose
To look at special beginnings connected with new year celebrations.

Activity 1: Thinking about the significance of a new year

A Ask the children how many times they may have heard someone say, 'I'm making a new year's resolution'. Put the word 'resolution' on the blackboard and explain its meaning.

B Discuss the kind of resolutions they could make that might please the children's parents and how such resolutions would also help themselves: to keep their bedroom tidy, to put toys away when they have finished with them, to wipe their feet when entering the house, to remember to put clothes away or out for washing, not to fight with brothers and sisters all the time, to work hard at school and so on. You may wish to remind the

children of the rules they have looked at (see **Beliefs and lifestyles**, p. 53) reinforcing how much happier we are when we have the discipline to live by them.

C Make a 'resolutions chart' for the classroom wall, with ideas on it. Discuss with the children whether there are any resolutions they feel they can keep up for a full 12-month period.

Activity 2: A new beginning for people with faith

A Explore the meaning of new year in the Hindu and Sikh faiths. Talk with the children about celebrating the new year as part of the Hindu Diwali festival when the door is left open for the goddess Lakshmi to enter, bringing good luck for the family in the year to come. Tell the children that before Lakshmi enters and the new year begins all Hindus are expected to settle their debts or accounts and the house must be clean and lit with *diva* lamps to welcome Lakshmi.

Inform the class that Baisakhi, the Sikh new year, is held in April and on this occasion the Sikh flag and flagpole are washed and rehung outside the gurdwara at a special ceremony. Sikh boys and girls and any adults who wish are baptised at the new year celebrations and begin new lives as Orthodox Sikhs.

On **Copymaster 70** (Faith and new beginnings) the children have to recognise in the pictures the goddess Lakshmi and the objects connected with the faith celebrations of Hinduism and Sikhism, reading the words at the bottom of the copymaster and filling in the blanks in the descriptions.

B Consider key moments in the children's own lives. Make individual books with the children called 'This is your life', looking at some shared dates and experiences, such as birthdays, school events and also the personal experiences special to the individual child. They can illustrate their books or stick photographs in place.

C Collect any special hymns or poems which emphasise the importance of the new day and look at them together. Discuss how the day can go well. Ask pupils if this would depend on the night before and how they felt when they got up that morning. Ask the children to consider the early morning prayers which Hindus, Muslims and Sikhs in particular are expected to make. Read them the following two descriptions:

● Savitri is a Hindu girl and she believes that it does help the new day to begin it with prayer.
'It helps me to concentrate my mind in a healthy way,' she says. 'Then if my little brother annoys me at breakfast time I'm a bit more patient with him – well, I think I am, anyway.'
● Philip is a Christian boy and his parents seem to find time to pray early in the morning.
'They don't make us join in,' says Philip. 'But it does help to make the day start properly.'

Talk with the children about these remarks and stress that, whatever happens at the beginning of a new day, the day is special because it *is* new and a fresh start for everyone. Examine the well-known prayer by Sir Philip Sidney: 'O Lord, you know how busy I will be today. If I forget you, don't forget me'.

D Pupils can write their own morning prayers which can be combined with work on other sections in this topic forming valuable material from which to produce a school assembly on the theme of creation and beginnings.

| Area of study 4 | **PEOPLE OF FAITH WHO FOUND NEW BEGINNINGS** |

Purpose
To give examples of people of faith from the past who found new beginnings.

Activity 1: How to make a fresh start
A Show the children pictures of ancient Rome and the Catacombs where Christians worshipped in secret, then show a photograph of a typical Roman citizen of 2 000 years ago.

The conversion of St Paul

B Read the story, **Paul travels to Damascus** (p. 81), and invite pupils to draw pictures of Paul on his travels, talking with Jesus on the way.
Now read the story **Sajjan the robber** (p. 81) to the children. Afterwards, they can act out the story and draw a picture of Sajjan meeting the Guru and Mardana at the inn when they arrived there as a backdrop to their play.

C Point out to the children that for both Paul and Sajjan there was a new beginning and ways in which they could start afresh and make up, as far as they were able, for the past. Can children give you any examples of others who have made new beginnings? Make a class list, then in groups pupils can construct banners showing figures who have made a new beginning in their lives. The banners can be made from stiff card and fastened at the back to long poles: they will make a colourful classroom/corridor display or can be used in a procession as part of your school assembly on this theme.

TOPIC STORIES

The creation story from Genesis

The earth was without any form or light so God created light and separated it from the darkness, calling the light 'day' and the darkness 'night'. This was the first day.

God said that there should be a vault separating the water. God called the vault 'Heaven'. This was the second day.

God made the moon and the stars to govern the night and the sun to govern the day on the fourth day.

On the fifth day, God made sea creatures and birds and ordered them to increase.

On the sixth day, God said that the earth should bring forth all living creatures. Then God created man in his own image, male and female and ordered them to rule over the living beings which moved on the earth.

God then blessed the seventh day and made it holy because on that day he finished all the work he had set himself.

The Hindu creation story

Before the world was made there was only the ocean and Lord Vishnu lay in the ocean, resting on a giant water snake which was coiled beneath him.

'I am ready to create the world,' Lord Vishnu decided, as he looked across the vast ocean.

Lord Brahma, the god of Creation, heard Lord Vishnu. He was sitting on a lotus flower waiting for Vishnu's command.

'I am ready now, Brahma,' said Lord Vishnu and Brahma divided the lotus flower on which he was sitting into three parts, heaven, sky and earth. On the earth he

placed plants of every kind, then animals and insects. On all these he breathed to give power of movement.

'Your world now needs someone to care for it and be happy in it,' Brahma told Lord Vishnu. He divided himself into two perfect beings, a woman called Shatarupa which means 'mysterious' and the other a man called Manu which means 'wise'. Shatarupa and Manu walked happily together into their beautiful world. They would perform the duty expected of every person who followed – to take care of Lord Vishnu's world.

Woman Fallen from the Sky

The very first people who existed lived beyond the sky and one day a girl fell through a hole in the sky. The girl was the daughter of the Chief of the first people.

Down and down the girl fell towards the endless water. She might have drowned but the beautiful swans broke her fall and held her safely on their backs until the great turtle came by to help them. He swam to the depths of the endless waters and heaped earth on his back. So World Island was created.

Woman Fallen from the Sky settled on World Island. Later her mother joined her because Woman Fallen from the Sky was going to have a baby and the wife of the Chief of the first people wanted to be with her daughter.

Woman Fallen from the Sky gave birth to twins, but later she died and the twins were brought up on World Island by their grandmother. One twin was good and the other twin was evil and it did not seem to matter how much Tsentsa, the good twin did because Taweskare, the bad one would undo it.

79

Tsentsa decided to create beautiful fertile land with gentle slopes but Taweskare produced swamps, chasms and bare mountain tops. When Tsentsa gave the land beautiful crops, trees and plants, Taweskare made the fruit smaller and covered it with prickly skins.

Noah and the rainbow

God told Noah to make a very special boat. It was to be a place of safety for Noah, his wife, their three sons and their wives, and a male and female animal, bird and reptile of every kind.

Noah trusted God but, even so, it was an unusual job to do and caused a lot of interest and curiosity among Noah's friends and neighbours.

'Where do you think you are going, Noah?' they called to Noah every day as the boat grew bigger and bigger. 'It must be a long trip. The boat's big enough.'

'God will be sending a flood all over the earth,' answered Noah. 'Come with me, if you like.'

The neighbours laughed at him. 'We've better things to do than to go sailing,' they said. 'It's a pity this is all you can find to do, Noah.'

Noah took no notice. God had told him exactly how he wanted the ark to be built and Noah and his three sons, Ham, Shem and Japheth, worked from morning until night to make the enormous boat big enough and waterproof.

At last the boat was ready.

'Round up the animals,' ordered Noah to his sons. 'As soon as we have two of every kind of animal, bird and reptile we can get into the ark and close the doors. 'You've got all the food, arranged, girls, haven't you?'

Noah's wife nodded. 'We've been getting it ready for days, Noah, and when Ham and Shem and Japheth have got time from rounding up the creatures they can load it all for us.'

At last the mountains of food were loaded into the ark and safely locked away. All down the road and for miles and miles stood the animals, from the much-loved dogs and cats owned by Noah and his family to lions, tigers and giraffes who towered above everyone. The birds were put into one of the recesses at the top of the boat and the reptiles were put next door to all the animals on the ground floor. Not all the animals wanted to go and Japheth, who was good with animals had to pull the difficult ones in by ropes.

Crowds of people watched the daily loading of the ark.

'There'll be no room for you, Noah,' they joked.

'Oh, there will – and room for you too, if you'll stop misbehaving and come with us,' replied Noah. 'You've been ignoring God and doing whatever you wanted for long enough.'

The crowds laughed and jeered until the last animal was on board and Noah, with a sad wave of the hands closed the doors and windows of the ark firmly.

Then the rains started. The people scattered and ran back to their homes. They thought the rain would stop but it didn't and soon the water was so deep that the ark lifted up and it seemed to sail away out of sight as some people tried to wade out after it. For a long time – forty days and nights – the water seemed to rise higher and higher and Noah gave strict orders that no windows should be opened.

At last the rain stopped and Noah's family crowded round him, begging him to let fresh air into the boat and open a window or a door.

'Fetch me one of the birds,' ordered Noah. 'We'll send him out. If he comes back, we'll know that the world is still under water.'

Japheth brought a black raven from the bird room upstairs in the ark. Noah opened one of the windows, took the bird gently from Japheth and put the raven through the window. Everyone waited and after a while the raven was back.

'We must keep on sailing,' said Noah to his disappointed family. 'It shouldn't be long before the waters begin to go down.'

Several days went by and then Noah asked Japheth to bring a dove to him. 'We'll try again,' he said. The dove, gently released through the window, was gone for some time. When she returned, she carried with her a leaf from a tree and then Noah and his family knew that the water was going down.

It was some time later that the boat suddenly hit something and everyone, Noah's family and all the animals and birds cried out in fright. Noah looked through the window. 'We're on top of the world,' he said. 'Look! We've landed on a mountain.'

As his family crowded to the window they could see they were high above the rest of the world, a lot of which was still covered in water.

'We can open the doors and all the windows and wait a little longer for the water to disappear completely,' said Noah.

'We could let the birds out,' said Japheth. 'They can rest in the trees.'

At last Noah and his family stepped out on to dry land. Mount Ararat, where they had landed would be a safe place for the boat to stay until Noah had decided where they should live. The animals were glad to be out and they began to run down the mountain to their new lives.

Noah stood for a while beside the Ark, talking with God who had chosen him and his family to begin the world again.

'Look up, Noah,' God seemed to say. 'I will never destroy the earth like this again. Look up in the clouds. There is my bow and my promise to the world that in future rain will stop and the world will be safe.'

Noah looked up at the sky. There, glistening and beautiful, was a rainbow. It was a new beginning.

Johnny's field

Johnny was a gardener at Ruskin Park in London. Next door to the park was a large hospital called King's College Hospital and the patients looked down on the park from their windows.

Until Johnny arrived, the large field below the hospital windows had become a rubbish dump. Visitors to the park threw cans and papers into it and nothing grew there.

Johnny changed all that. He took away all the rubbish, turned the soil over and planted the most beautiful flowers which would bloom in every season of the year.

No one knew that Johnny was really a sick man and one day he became so ill that he had to be rushed to the big hospital by the park. As Johnny looked down from the window of his room, the flowers seemed to glow more brightly and they seemed to say, 'This is for you, Johnny. We are growing brighter every day.'

Johnny died soon afterwards but that beautiful field, which in the winter has magnificent snowdrops, is alive with golden daffodils in spring and in the summer is ablaze with many colours, will always be known as 'Johnny's field'.

Paul travels to Damascus

Paul was a Roman citizen and his real name was Saul. When Jesus' disciples began to hold special Christian meetings in Jerusalem, Paul did his very best to stop them. He went to the homes of any Christians he could find, dragged them in chains through the streets and threw them into prison. Therefore, Christians had to meet secretly under the city of Jerusalem itself in caves known as 'catacombs' below the streets.

Some Christians escaped to the city of Damascus and Paul found out about this. He asked the Jewish leaders if he could take some soldiers to Damascus and capture all Christians he found there.

On the way to Damascus Paul suddenly became blind and he heard Jesus' voice asking him, 'Why are you persecuting me?' The other soldiers thought their Captain was very ill indeed and they took him to a house in Damascus. Paul lay, blind and not eating and drinking anything for days.

A Christian in Damascus called Ananias was asked by God to go to Paul and heal him. Ananias was frightened and at first he didn't want to go because he thought Paul would have him killed. In the end he did go and when he saw Paul, Ananias felt sorry for him. He placed his hands on Paul's eyes and Paul's sight came back.

Ananias talked to Paul about Jesus and because of his experience on the road to Damascus, Paul believed in Jesus and was baptised as a Christian.

Not many Christians believed at first that Paul had become one of them but Paul soon proved to them that he meant every word he said. Paul became the most important Christian missionary of all time.

Sajjan the robber

Guru Nanak, the founder of the Sikh faith, often travelled through dangerous countryside. One evening he and his friend, Mardana, wanted somewhere to stay for the night and they enquired in the area where Guru Nanak was preaching.

'There's Sajjan's place,' someone said, but other people gave cries of horror. 'Don't send the guru there,'

they cried. 'Sajjan is a murderer and a thief. The guru and his friend will never come out alive.'

'Tell me more about Sajjan,' said Guru Nanak and the people explained that Sajjan had an unusual inn with a Hindu temple and a mosque attached to it.

'Because of the places of worship many people go there but if they are rich they never come out alive,' they said.

'Well, I'm not rich,' smiled Guru Nanak.

'No, but you are well-known and Sajjan will think you are rich,' Nanak was told.

'I think I'd better go and see if I can do anything to soften this man's heart,' decided Nanak. 'Don't worry, Mardana,' he added, noticing how frightened his friend was. 'We'll be alright.'

Guru Nanak and Mardana reached Sajjan's inn at about 6 o'clock. Everything was quiet and Guru Nanak thought it may be because 6 o'clock was the time for Hindu and Muslim prayers. Then Sajjan appeared, dressed in rich clothes and welcomed his visitors warmly.

'What would you like to eat?' he asked.

'Oh, I'll wait until your other guests eat,' answered Guru Nanak. 'If you will show us to our rooms we will bathe before our meal.'

'Haven't you brought any luggage with you?' asked Sajjan in surprise.

'No,' said Guru Nanak, staring hard at Sajjan. 'Our possessions are in a friend's home until we return.'

Nanak and Mardana were shown to their rooms which were comfortable. They had not been there long when Sajjan's servant arrived at Guru Nanak's room with some food which smelled so good that Mardana wanted to eat it.

'Thank you,' Nanak said to the servant, who bowed and left them.

'Don't touch it, Mardana,' warned Guru Nanak. 'We will eat later when I have sorted this out. Now first we must put the food off the plates and pretend we've eaten it.'

Mardana grumbled but Guru Nanak emptied the food into an old piece of sacking he found in a cupboard in the room.

'Now we lie down and pretend to be asleep,' said Nanak.

They lay there with their eyes closed for some time and then they heard the door of their room open softly.

'They're asleep, Master,' said the servant to Sajjan. 'Shall we kill them now?'

Guru Nanak sat up at once.

'It is as I thought, Sajjan,' he said sternly. 'That food was poisoned. You thought you would kill us and take any money we have as you have done with your other guests. No wonder there's no one else here. You've killed them all.'

Sajjan didn't know what to do. Someone was already knocking at his door and when Nanak looked out of the window, he saw some of the people he had met that day. They had come to see if it was alright. Guru Nanak opened the window and told the anxious people he was alright. Then he said to Sajjan, 'You and I are going to have a talk.'

There was nothing Sajjan could do to bring back all the people he had killed but he did have a bit of money and Guru Nanak insisted that this should go to the relatives of the people who had lost their lives.

'And you will come with me,' said Nanak. 'I have work for you to do.'

Sajjan was deeply ashamed and sorry for all he had done. He threw open his inn as a free place for travellers to stay and eventually he became a well-known Sikh missionary, the first one after Guru Nanak to travel about the country speaking about the Sikh faith.

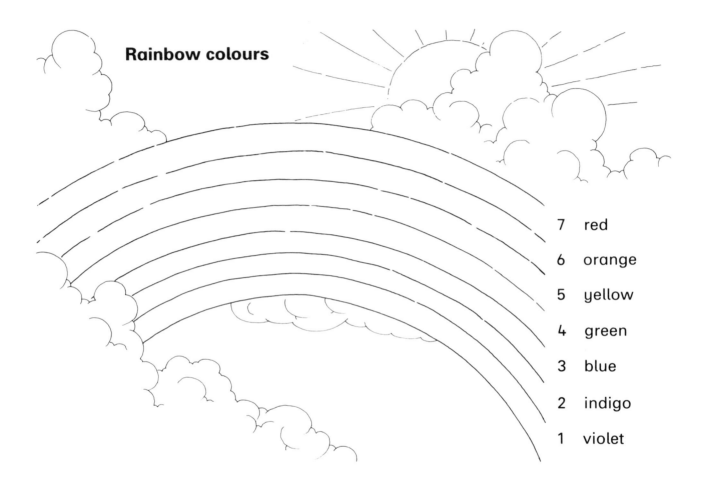

Rainbow colours

7 red

6 orange

5 yellow

4 green

3 blue

2 indigo

1 violet

The natural world

The four elements

- Earth, air and fire – how they affect us
- Focus on water
- How water is used in a religious context

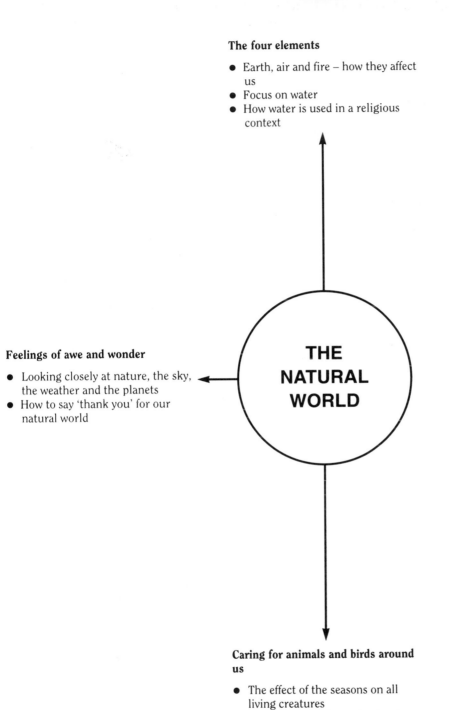

THE NATURAL WORLD

Feelings of awe and wonder

- Looking closely at nature, the sky, the weather and the planets
- How to say 'thank you' for our natural world

Caring for animals and birds around us

- The effect of the seasons on all living creatures
- How to help birds survive in winter

LEARNING OBJECTIVES

- To become more aware of those aspects of the world which will arouse feelings of mystery, awe, wonder, pleasure and sadness.
- To encourage a variety of responses to these aspects of the natural world by using story, music, art, drama and poetry.
- To use stories from several faiths which give examples of people who have (and are showing) the development of links between themselves and the natural world.
- To consider such festivals as Rogation (blessing of crops) and Harvest, to show ways in which human beings link with God and give thanks for the production of crops.

STARTING POINTS

- Explain to the children what a natural element in our world is. Give them an example such as water. Ask them if they can think of other natural elements, namely earth, fire and air. Write these words down on the blackboard.

- Ask the children to think of examples when we use these elements in our everyday lives around us. Some examples might be switching on the light in the classroom, running a tap in the kitchen at home or in the cloakroom at school, responding to the teacher's blown whistle at the end of playtime. Explain that we rely upon these elements to live and survive in our world.

- Show the children pictures of some of the elements such as the sun, a fountain, a volcano, a rainbow, birds singing. Ask them to name the elements represented in these pictures. Then ask them if they have ever thought about how much we need or depend upon them to live. Ask them if they have ever thought about how amazing the world is in which we live. What do they think is amazing about the world?

- Ask the children to make their own list, 'The things in the world that I think are amazing'. Look at these lists with them, concentrating on one or two examples and make the point that without these elements our world could not exist.

- Ask the children if they say 'thank you' for the world in which they live. Who do they say thank you to?

- Learn the topic song, **Natural World**, which can be sung in a special assembly on this theme.

THE FOUR ELEMENTS

Area of study 1

C71 –75

Purpose
To look at the four elements in our natural world and examine how they affect our lives.

Activity 1: Earth, air and fire
Remind the children of the four elements you all named in **Starting points**. Write them in big letters on large cards in different colours (earth in green felt-tip, air in grey, and fire in red). Explain you are going to look at these elements first and how they affect us.

Earth
[A] Look at a globe with the children. Ask them what shape the earth is. What does the blue colour on the globe represent? Inform them that our earth is made up of water and ice, areas of land of which a fifth is mountain area, an eighth is desert and a quarter is forest. Get a child to point to the coldest places on the earth and another child to point to the hottest places. Say that all this makes up our natural world. They can then look for our country on the globe and you can work out how big it is in relation to the rest of the world.

[B] Give the children a world map (you may wish to copy Copymaster 50) and ask them to colour the earth in green and the water in blue. Ask them if they can tell you what there is more of on the earth – land or water?

[C] Hold up a piece of chalk and say it is a type of rock. Explain that rocks form a large part of our natural world and are made up of shells of tiny sea creatures which lived many millions of years ago. Arrange a display of different types of rock and ask the children to observe them, noticing colour, shape and texture. The children can then draw, name and colour them in on a large sheet of paper. At the bottom of the sheet of paper, they can write a few lines to say that rock was once liquid, deep inside the earth before cooling and setting on the earth's surface.

D Ask pupils if there is a river near where they live. Can they think of any names of famous rivers of the world? Go back to the world map and have a look: can they find any on the globe?

Point out that these rivers begin as small streams that eventually get bigger and bigger and then run into the sea. Play them the music *The Moldau* by Smetana, which depicts a tiny stream travelling across country and joining the sea.

After hearing the music children can make a wall frieze showing the river's journey, running down slopes and polishing stones, passing through the countryside, alongside houses and people on its way to the sea. Use as many materials as possible and display along a school corridor. Introduce words such as 'tributary' and 'estuary' and write these words on cards which can be placed at appropriate points on the wall frieze.

E Get the children to write a story about a little stream who has many adventures before its eventual arrival at the sea. What did it feel like when it arrived there?

F Ask the children to find pictures for themselves of land such as fields, mountains, forests and deserts. They can discuss together what they can see in the pictures. Suggest that they compile a simple card index (each card being A4-sized) called 'Our earth' which could contain the world map they have been referring to, short poems about the world drawings in felt-tip, pastel and crayon of all the characteristics of the natural world they have been looking at, and some basic facts about each: for example, 'Dry desert covers nearly one eighth of our land area'. Ensure that each card is given a title and filed alphabetically: you can help pupils to refer to their index throughout the topic.

Ask children to colour in the globe on **Copymaster 71** (Natural world) showing the land as green and the sea blue. They should then complete the blanks which describe the pictures, using the words at the bottom of the copymaster.

Air
A Introduce the second element, air, by asking the children what it is they breathe in. Remind them that all living creatures need air (oxygen) in which to breathe and that air is all around us even though we cannot see, taste or smell it. Tell them we can all learn about air by observing what it does around us and how it affects us.

B Ask pupils to write about what it feels like to walk down the street on a windy day. Discuss with them the describing words they have chosen. What other examples can they think of where air affects things? Make a list of these such as trees blowing, washing on the line, a candle flame flickering, etc.

C Whip cream in front of the children, using a hand whisk or electric hand whisk, and demonstrate how bubbles of air transform the look and texture of the cream making it very light and fluffy.

D Give a child a paper windmill and ask them to walk across the classroom. It is likely that the children will know that the sails will move, but ask them if they know why and how. Explain that it is moving through the air that causes the sails to move.

✓ Give out **Copymaster 72** (How do they fall?) Children should observe and record the way different objects fall through the air. They can read the names on the copymaster and draw a picture of each object. After letting the object fall, they note on the sheet the way in which it falls and the speed – 'quick' or 'slow', etc. Lastly, ask them to listen carefully as the object lands on the ground and write on the sheet whether the sound was soft, loud or inaudible.

E Look at a picture of a bird in flight with the children. They should look closely at its wings and observe what they look like. Ask them to mime the action of a bird flying with their arms and say why its wings beat downwards. The children can imagine they are a bird flying in the sky, right over where they live, and write a short simple poem about what it feels like to be flying through the air and what they can see below and around them because they are able to fly. Create atmosphere by playing music such as Debussy, Delius and Vaughan Williams and ask children to combine elements of dance and mime to perform flight sequences.

F Look at pictures of air travel such as helicopters, aeroplanes, hot-air balloons, and so on. Investigate with the children what it is that enables these machines to fly by looking closely at the shape and structure of the machines. Pupils can make a paper aeroplane and colour a design on it. They can take it in turns to 'launch' the aeroplanes, taking care when throwing them so that they lift into the air. Ask them to measure and compare the distances travelled.

Fire flashcards

G Use **Copymaster 73** (Air travel) to name and label three types of air travel, using the words at the bottom of the copymaster.

Make the children aware of the fact that as well as big machines flying through the air, tiny flies in our world also need air to fly through. Explain that a fly beats its wings 1 000 times a second and watch the movement. Ask them if they can think of any other insects that have powerful wings with which they fly through the air – bees, wasps, dragonflies, butterflies, etc.

H Look at the effect strong winds have on nature. Ask them what happens to leaves on trees or delicate roses in gardens on a windy autumn day.

I Ask the children to close their eyes and imagine the sound of thunder. What words can they tell you to describe this sound? Write them down on the blackboard or on a flipchart for the children to see. Ask them what is happening to cause the sound and the clash of warmth and cool air high up in the sky.

Pupils can write a short description of a hot, summer day when the weather alters and a thunderstorm is coming, describing the change in the air as the storm gathers by using interesting words and noting people's reactions .

Fire

A Introduce the third element, fire, by asking the children to close their eyes and imagine they are standing at the scene of a bonfire on Bonfire Night. Ask them to tell you what the bonfire looks like and give you a list of vivid descriptive words. They can compile poems from the words describing the colour, light, sparks, bangs and crackles at a bonfire party. Encourage them to work imaginatively by producing the words they have thought of on separate flashcards in appropriate shapes and colours: cards could be flame-shaped, firework-shaped, cloud-shaped or flash-shaped, etc. as in the illustration above.

B Ask the children to think about fire and what it makes them feel like. Tell them you are sure that they are excited when they go to a bonfire on Bonfire Night and that some people light bonfires at other times for other celebratory reasons. Give an example, such as the Hindu spring festival, Holi, where all Hindus light a bonfire in the evening and come together in friendship to welcome the spring and new beginnings.

C Explain the use of candles as part of celebration at festivals like advent and Christingle. **Copymaster 74** (Natural glow) can be used by pupils to make their own celebratory candle. Children can use wax crayons of two different colours and draw stripes across or down the rectangle. They can then scrape a pattern on to the wax if they wish. (The rectangle is measured to fit around a toilet roll with an overlap of half an inch for glueing.) Cut out some gold paper the size of the flame on the copymaster and position on the sheet. Colour the circle red or cut out shiny red paper the size of the circle and stick on the copymaster. Cut out the rectangle, the flame and the circle. Stick the rectangle around the toilet roll and glue the flame into position at the top edge of the toilet roll using the square shape to secure it. Fix the red circle on to stiff card and use as a stand for the candle.

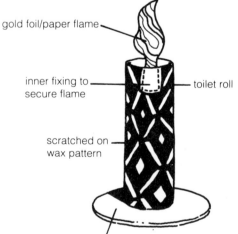

gold foil/paper flame

inner fixing to secure flame

toilet roll

scratched on wax pattern

cardboard circle (stand)

D Ask the children when fire is not such a welcome guest. Can they give some examples? How do they feel when they hear a fire engine racing down the road with its sirens wailing and its blue light flashing? Does it worry them where the fire is and if anyone might be hurt? Ask them if fire makes them feel frightened or excited, or do they just like to think about its warmth and light? Ask them to write a poem called 'Fire makes

me feel . . .'. They can paint a border surrounding their poems, using bright colours connected with fire.

E The children can make posters depicting the dangers of fire and containing a short, sharp message about how to prevent it: for example, unguarded fires, chip pans on fire, a discarded match, etc.

Visit the local fire station with your class. Take the fire posters along and show them to the officers. Talk to the officers about the different engines, the fire-fighting equipment and the uniform. Alternatively, ask the fire officer to come into school to talk to your class about fire and why a fire drill is so necessary in school. Ask the children to look closely at the firefighter's uniform. Afterwards ask them what would happen if the firefighters did not wear these special uniforms. How would fire affect them then?

F Make pottery or Plasticine® models of a fireman, a fire station or a fire engine. Remind the children that pottery models have to be fired in a kiln of simple brick-built structure, and that the temperature has to be very high to 'bake' their models.

Activity 2: The element water

Water everywhere

A Sit with the children informally and begin by asking them to shout out some words that come into their heads when they think of water. Ask them what colour water is; does it have a shape and does it taste or smell of anything? Explain that water is everywhere, found in more places and things than they had perhaps realised.

B Bring samples of fruit into school. Give a child a pear, another an apple, another a melon, and so on. Ask each child to bite into the fruit and tell you what comes out of it. The children will say 'juice': tell them that the juice from fruit is mostly made up of water.

C Ask pupils to note down as many uses of water as they can and then select one item from their list to form the basis of a 'water wheel' made from stiff card with their message written around the edge. A central hole

should be made so that when a pencil is pushed through the centre, children can watch their wheel spin.

Use **Copymaster 75** (We need water for . . .) to reinforce how vital water is for our daily/weekly routines. Children can match the correct job to each picture. Make a list with the children of rooms in which water is found in our homes. Discuss what it is used for and then write this down. Pupils can then cut out pictures of bathrooms and kitchens from magazines and illustrate their writing with these.

Give the children a title for a class mime called 'What I do with water in the home'. Divide the class into groups and give each group an activity like 'cleaning', or 'brushing my teeth' and say to each group they must keep their activity a secret. Each group can then mime the activity in turn in front of the others who have to guess what the activity is.

D Show the children a wide variety of colour pictures of water outside the home such as rain, streets after it has rained, the seaside. Ask the children to draw pictures of people affected by water outside the home. This could be a picture of a child getting wet going to school, a wet postman, milkman, lollipop man or lady. Underneath the pictures, the children can briefly describe how the water affects these people in their daily tasks.

E Ask the children why Mum or Dad hangs the washing outside on the line when the washing is damp and wet. They will easily tell you 'to dry' but ask them if they have ever thought about where the water goes to. Explain simply that water evaporates and when the sky becomes too full of water it has to rain. Divide a poster-size sheet of paper into four sections and invite pupils to make four large pictures depicting Mum hanging out the washing, little droplets of water escaping from the washing into the air, lots of clouds forming made up of these tiny droplets and lastly, rainfall itself. Arrange the pictures side by side on the classroom wall and above them put a large title 'Water travels'.

F Read the children the story **The little stream** (p. 92) as an example of the problems that can arise if there is not enough water. Explain that the little stream could not survive without the rain to fill it up again, stressing we all need rain even if we do think it is a nuisance getting wet on the way to and from school!

G Show the children a bottle of spring water. Tell them that this is pure, clean water. Then show the children a picture of a river. Tell them the river might look pretty but some people will have dumped rubbish or dangerous products into it. Explain that water is a precious substance wherever it is found and we must not pollute it like this. Ask them if they had ever thought about how raindrops carry fumes and smoke back to earth: this can harm our natural world so we must also be careful not to pollute the air. This would be a good opportunity to make environment posters with the message that the whole world needs water and we must keep it clean. Alternatively, display a variety of reference books on the survival of plants and animals and ask the children to look up all the ways fish and plants need water to survive.

H Obtain a miniature model of a person which shows internal parts of the body (blood, muscle, bone). Ask pupils if they know where water may be found in the body and how much there is. Inform them that our bodies need water in order to function properly and this is why people become ill quickly in countries where there is a shortage of water. Pupils can make mobiles called 'We all need water' showing parts of the human body, fish, plants, fruit, animals, etc., suspended from the ceiling on different lengths of cotton.

I Look at pictures of the sea with the children. Show them the sea on a grey, stormy day and on a calm, clear day. Ask them what colour the sea is in the pictures. Read them the story **At the seaside** (p. 92) illustrating that water has no colour and therefore the sea has no colour either but is only reflecting the colour of the sky.

Following on from this, look again at the two sea pictures and talk about how such a large quantity of water can affect people's lives, pointing out that the sea is very powerful. Look at the work of the fisherman, sailor, lifeboatman and read the story The lifeboat (p. 92) about the power of the sea and the dangers of the waters if people do not heed warnings given. Children can write short descriptions of the people whose work is

connected with the sea and what they do (the fisherman, sailor, lifeboatmen, coastguards, etc.). Pupils can write a class letter inviting a representative of the coastguard to visit the school and talk about their work.

How water is used in a religious context

A Ask the children to bring in photographs of a family baptism or show them colourful pictures from books of a baptism taking place in a church. Ask them if they know what it is that the water is kept in. Remind the pupils of their visit to the local church (**Birth celebrations**, p. 41) and point out particularly the position of the font. Why do they think the water has to be placed in this special font? Explore the meaning of baptism together and the significance of the use of water for the ceremony.

B Tell the children about John the Baptist and read the description from the Bible where he is seen baptising people (John 1:26). Point out that many people today are baptised in this way and fully immersed in water. Show them photographs of this taking place.

C Write down the words 'baptism', 'font', 'water', 'minister', 'priest' and 'baby' on large cards and show these to the children. They can then paint or draw pictures of a baptism and label the pictures using these words.

CARING FOR ANIMALS AND BIRDS AROUND US

Purpose
To examine the effect of the seasons on all living creatures and what we can do to help birdlife in winter.

Activity 1: The seasons
A Arrange a mixture of coloured dried leaves, small flowers, pebbles and buds or twigs on a large table. Gather the children around the table and talk about the colours of each object. Ask them what seasons we might

associate with these colours. The children can make miniature season pictures using the objects.

B The children can then write short descriptions or poems on the seasons and the way the seasons make them feel (cold, hot, happy, full of life, etc.).

C Sit the children informally and ask them if they have ever thought about how animals and birds are affected by the seasons. Show them a picture of birds returning in springtime from a warmer climate where they have had to go because of our cold winter; a tortoise who has weakened from hibernation; birds collecting materials for building nests and preening their feathers. Make a spring tree collage, putting in the tree birds and animals who are busy making new homes in the spring and singing spring songs.

[D] Show the children several colour pictures of animals and insects in summertime such as a dog panting, an animal with young, butterflies and other insects feeding from flowers in bloom, and so on. Ask the children to tell you in which season these animals and insects are seen in this way.

[E] Make a display of acorns, nuts and berries and discuss what these are with the children and who will be looking for them to store away and eat throughout the winter. Compile a chart on which the children can fill in the natural foods and the name of the animal who will be searching for them to store away for the coming winter.

[F] Ask pupils to close their eyes and imagine a field covered with a blanket of snow. Explain that this blanket helps to keep things warmer for longer under the ground in winter. Help the children to make a wall frieze showing mice, voles and other small creatures living underground. Include a pond or lake and show fish surviving in water under a layer of ice.

[G] Read the story **The cat in the woodshed** (p. 93) to the children explaining that we must all keep our eyes open for animals around us and make sure that they are not in difficulty.

Activity 2: How to help birds survive in winter
[A] Remind the children of the creatures you have just been looking at who are fortunate enough to survive the winter under a layer of snow or ice. Explain they are the lucky ones because there are many who find it difficult to survive the winter. Tell them that you are all going to look at the ways in which birds who remain in this country can be helped in wintertime. Get the children to identify some birds they see every day.

[B] The children can draw a bird table and say what it is made out of. Discuss a design in detail. Would the

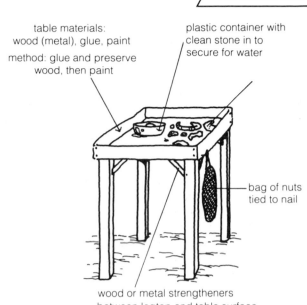

table materials: wood (metal), glue, paint
method: glue and preserve wood, then paint

plastic container with clean stone in to secure for water

bag of nuts tied to nail

wood or metal strengtheners between legtop and table surface

table need to have a lip or ledge on which the birds can balance? How tall would the table be? What sort of drink could be placed on the table and in what type of container?

[C] Bring into school scraps of food suitable for birds to eat. Make a recipe in which all the scraps can be mixed together to make a tasty pudding for the birds. Write the recipe on a card and illustrate it. If there is time, make the food in front of the children.

[D] A string of nuts can be made by threading them together in a row. Discuss where the string could be hung for easy feeding by the birds. Create a bird bath out of a suitable container. Let pupils decide where this should be placed in the school grounds: remind them that the water has to be watched to keep it clean and when frozen it should be melted by pouring warm water into the bird bath.

[E] The children can write a poem or short description about birds assembling at a bird table for a tasty meal and refreshing drink and gathering at bathtime at a bird bath. Show them words on flashcards to help them describe the birds' actions such as 'splashing', 'pecking', 'chasing', 'calling', etc.

Area of study 3 — FEELINGS OF AWE AND WONDER ▶

Purpose
To look carefully at and admire the beauty of God's world, focusing on nature, the weather, the sky and the planets and how to say 'thank you' for our natural world.

Activity 1: Looking closely at nature – the sky, the weather and the planets
[A] Take the children to a local park and ask them to look around and tell you what they see (trees, flowers,

grass, plants). Tell them that nature is all around us and to appreciate it fully we must look closely to find out more about it.

✓ Take **Copymaster 76** (Park survey) with you. Pupils should look for objects in the park listed on the copymaster and place a tick in the boxes when they have been observed, totalling the number of the same object in the circle at the end of each line.

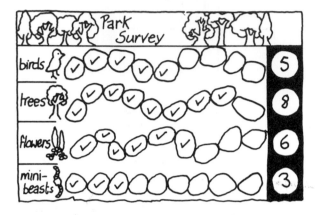

The children can look at trees in small groups and take rubbings, describing the appearance and the feel of the bark. They can press their ears against the trunks and listen for the 'heartbeat': explain to them that this is water moving from the roots under the ground up the trunk and out towards the leaves.

Examine the leaves together, their colour, texture and shape. Ask the children if the leaves feel moist or damp to touch. Explain that they feel damp because of water in the leaves. (Demonstrate this in school by placing a plastic bag over a leaf they have collected and fasten it securely. Ask the children to observe what happens. They should see water from the leaf appearing on the inside of the bag.)

B Look at plants with the children. Explain they need light to grow as well as air and water. Pupils can experiment with seeds (cress or bean) and watch growth occurring when they are placed in glass jars, recording the various stages of growth by drawing the seeds and describing what is happening.

Demonstrate how to make a bottle garden. Include a variety of plants and point out what is needed for the plants to grow inside the bottle. The children can keep a record of the plants' growth.

Allocate an area of the school grounds where pupils can grow their own wildflower garden or alternatively cultivate plants in a miniature garden area in the classroom. Invite the children to take cuttings and collect seeds for future growth.

C Look at real flowers with the children. Examine them closely and talk about the different parts. Show them the names of these parts on flashcards. Make model flowers with the children out of coloured tissue paper. Talk about the amazing colours and the delicacy of a flower. Pressed or dried flowers can be used to create attractive and unusual pictures.

D Look at photographs of the countryside, of fields and different grasses. Point out that fields as well as looking beautiful also provide food for cattle, and homes for birds, butterflies and insects who are also looking for food. The children can make calendars and record on them what happens at different times of the year (when grasses flower, when hay is cut in fields and put into bundles, etc.)

E Take the children outside and look at the sky, asking them what they see. Write these words down in the classroom and ask the children to describe the sky in their own words. Have they ever wondered why the sky is blue? Explain to them this is because there are blue light rays from the sun. Go on to discuss why the sky is red when the sun sets. Ask the children to paint pictures of a blue sky and a red sky and position the sun correctly.

Look at pictures of the sky at night with the children and ask them to tell you exactly what they can see in the picture. Do they realise that stars are always in the sky even though they seem to disappear in the daytime? The children can write descriptions of the sky at night and how they feel when they look up at the sky at this time.

F Ask the children if they can tell you what the weather is like outside. Study with them the differences that occur when the weather is hot and when it is dry. Show them colour pictures or photographs of rainy and sunny places. With the help of **Copymaster 77** (How much rain?), ask them to collect rainwater in a jar over a period of a week measuring every day how much rain has fallen. Results should be recorded by drawing the level of rainfall on the jars, shading beneath the line and writing the number of millilitres on the front of the jar. At the end of the week the children can fill in the bar graph.

G Distribute **Copymasters 78** and **79** (Seasonal cards 1 and 2). Use four pieces of A4-sized card for backing and make each seasonal card one at a time. Look at

	MONDAY	TUESDAY	WEDNESDAY	THURSDAY	FRIDAY
AM	SUNNY SPELLS	RAIN			
PM	SUNNY				
PM PREDICTION	CLOUDY	CLOUDY			

Compiling a weather chart

Copymaster 78 and discuss it. Choose a season: for example, winter. Cut out the label 'winter', the figure underneath and the weather symbol underneath that. Arrange on stiff, coloured card (perhaps grey) in this order. Look at the pictures of winter clothes in the boxes on Copymaster 79 and the corresponding words underneath. Cut out the winter clothes and words and arrange next to the figure on the seasonal card. Finally, children should draw in the clothes on the figure using items given on Copymaster 78 as a guide.

H Go and stand with the children in sunshine. Ask them to describe to you what it feels like. Does the warmth of the sun make them feel happy? Now take the children out on to the school playing field. Show them how to fly a kite. Let them take it in turns to hold the strings and point out the force of the wind which keeps the kite aloft. How do the children feel when the wind is blowing them? Ask them to describe this and draw a picture of themselves on a windy day. They can then draw pictures of other things affected by the wind such as trees with the leaves falling and washing on a line.

Follow up the theme of movement by dividing the class into groups giving each group a bowl half-filled with water and each child a straw. Ask the children to blow down the straw across the surface of the water and then notice what happens. Mention the words 'ripples' and 'movement'. The children can then describe the experiment and write down what happens to water when the wind blows.

I Tell the children that they can all turn into 'weather girls' and 'weather boys' and predict the weather by looking at clouds. Take them outside and learn about the different types of clouds which tell us what the weather will be like. In the classroom they can paint the different types and each day they can take it in turns to predict what the weather will be like for the morning and again for the afternoon while they are in school. The children can keep a weather diary and record the weather for the week both in it and on a weather chart on a classroom wall which they can make themselves as shown above. They can also make a weather book and in it describe how amazing the weather really is in terms of its power to provide and

destroy, but however it affects us, it is a part of our natural world greatly needed for survival.

J Explain to the class that they are now going to look at marvels beyond the sky: marvels which they cannot actually see but which exist. Show the children a picture of the earth and the position of the planets in relation to it. Carry out a brief study of selected planets, noting details such as their size, colour, shape and what scientists have discovered about them so far. Invite pupils to paint pictures of the planets and make a 'Planet corner' in the classroom where these studies and pictures can be displayed. A collage for the wall can also be made showing that all the children have understood about what there is beyond the sky. In a progression from the bottom upwards, show a blue sky, mist effect, darkness, stars/small planets, larger planets and meteorites or satellites.

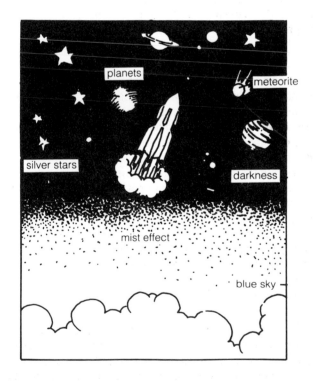

K Ask the children to paint a picture of an imaginary planet, one that might be part of our natural world but no one has discovered yet. They can write an imaginary

91

story about a visit to this newly-discovered planet describing it and the forms of life that exist there.

L Play music which is descriptive of the planets, notably *The Planets Suite* by Gustav Holst. The children can experiment with percussion instruments and make their own space music. Does their music sound mysterious, exciting, happy? Do they find this unknown part of our natural world wonderful too? Encourage them to talk about this and write creatively about what they feel in the form of a short descriptive piece of writing.

M Ask the children to write a poem which includes everything they have looked at in this Area of Study, namely nature, the sky, the weather and the planets. They can write a verse on each emphasising feelings of wonder and amazement at God's creation. The poem could be called 'Amazing creation'.

Activity 2: How to say 'thank you' for our natural world

A Tell the children that our natural world should not be taken for granted and that we should be grateful for it, taking care of it in the best ways we can. Ask them to think about how we can say 'thank you' for the marvellous gifts it provides. Create an assembly on the natural world, to include some of their artwork, stories and poems and when they can sing the topic song. Tell them they are thanking God by doing all this and that the rest of the class will also be thanking him on assembly day by joining in through singing and praying together.

B The children can make a comprehensive book of prayers, some of which can be used in the assembly. Help the children to focus their ideas by making a list of things they wish to say thank you for:

- the sea, sky, planets – the world in which we live
- all living creatures – birds, insects, animals
- earth, air, fire, water – without these we could not live
- each other – our families, friends and classmates

Copymaster 80 (My thankyou prayer) will help pupils to write a prayer of thanks to God for the natural world. They should write within the circle around which some words appear to remind the children of what they have learnt about in this topic. They can draw a picture or decorative border around the circle edge and then cut it out. All the prayers can be collected together and made into their large, circular class book of prayers. On the front of the book could be a picture of the earth and the planets shown positioned around it.

C Remind the children that they can also show their gratitude to God for the natural world by taking care of it, not only by looking after their local environment but by helping to preserve other parts of the world by giving their time to help raise money for the poorer countries through charity work. Discuss ways in which this can be done so the world can remain a beautiful and breathtaking place for everyone.

TOPIC STORIES ▶

The little stream
The little stream was upset. The sun had been shining for many days and he was beginning to dry up.

'When the children come to play they say "There's hardly any water in this stream" and go away again,' the little stream said sadly. 'Oh, I do wish it would rain.'

'What about us?' whispered the wild flowers, which grew by the edge of the stream. 'We have to have water or we will die.'

The stream grew smaller and smaller and the meadow flowers grew more thirsty.

'Mr Oak Tree, can't you do something?' croaked the little stream. 'You are nearer to the sky than any of us. Ask a friendly cloud to help us.'

'I can try,' said the tree. He sent a message to his topmost branches and they asked the clouds for help.

Nothing happened for a while, but during the night, when the sun was asleep, the clouds sent the rain. It poured down on to the thirsty flowers and plants, and it poured into the little stream so much that he almost overflowed. The little stream rushed proudly along the countryside again.

At the seaside
Timmy and Helen were playing at the seaside with their mother.

'Let's go down to the beach,' their mother said the first morning. So Timmy carried his bucket and spade and a football. Helen carried her bucket and spade and a beach ball. Mother carried a bag with Helen's swimsuit, Timmy's swimming trunks, two large towels and some cold drinks and food inside it.

When they got to the sea, it was blue.

'What a lovely colour,' said Helen.

'Why is the sea so blue today?' asked Timmy, as he kicked his football along the sand.

'Because the sky is blue,' answered his mother. 'The sea is always the same colour as the sky.'

'Sometimes the sea is grey,' Timmy said.

'If the sky is grey the sea is grey,' Helen told him. 'Water has no colour of its own.'

The lifeboat
The sea can be calm and peaceful, but it can also be rough and dangerous. Many ships have been lost at sea in stormy weather.

Every seaside resort and every port has a team of brave people who sail out to sea in a special boat to save people in danger. This special boat is known as a lifeboat because it saves people's lives.

Helen and Timmy loved the seaside and the beach, but their father was a lifeboat man and he told them to be very careful.

'The sea can be gentle and calm,' he told them. 'But it can be fierce and rough and cruel as well. Watch out for the "danger" signs on the beach.'

This is why Helen and Timmy hurried back to the safe part of the beach as soon as they saw the 'danger – high tide' sign.

The cat in the woodshed

Roger was the first to arrive in the schoolyard and he kicked a stone around for a while, wishing that his friends would hurry up. His mother had to bring him to school early because she had to take Roger's little sister, Tracy, to their Gran's before she went to her job at the supermarket.

'It can't be helped, Roger,' his mother said every morning when he grumbled about always being at school before anyone else. 'You want that bike for your birthday, don't you? Well, I've got to go to work to be able to buy presents like that.'

Suddenly the little boy heard some calling to him. It was a woman passing by the school gate. Roger had been told not to talk to strangers but the woman was pointing to the small woodshed at the side of the school building. Roger ran over to her and the woman was still pointing at the shed.

'I can hear a cat crying,' she told Roger. 'I'm sure it's locked inside that shed. I've got to go to work. Can you do something about it?'

Roger listened at the door of the woodshed. Sure enough a faint crying could be heard. 'I can hear the cat, too,' he said. 'I'll get someone.' The woman nodded and hurried away.

Roger thought quickly. Miss Stewart, the head teacher, was just getting out of her car by the school gate and Roger ran over to her.

'Hello, Roger. Early as usual.' Miss Stewart smiled at him as she locked her car door.

'Miss Stewart, there's a cat locked in the woodshed,' Roger blurted out. 'Can you come, please?'

Miss Stewart followed Roger to the shed and listened carefully.

'Oh, yes. I can hear it,' she said at last. 'Do you know where Mr Robinson's room is, Roger?'

Mr Robinson was the caretaker and his room was at the far end of the Infant School building.

'Yes, Miss. I know where it is. I'll go and tell him,' Roger answered and he ran into the building and down the corridor until he found the caretaker who was drinking tea in his little room.

'Mr Robinson, can you come, please? A cat's got stuck in the woodshed.' Roger didn't stop for breath when the caretaker opened his door to him.

'Alright, son. I'll come now.'

Mr Robinson took a large key from a nail behind his door and followed Roger back along the corridor and into the yard where Miss Stewart was standing with a group of children.

The caretaker unlocked the woodshed door and opened it. Miss Stewart told all the children to stand back.

'Look.' Mr Robinson beckoned to Roger. Inside the woodshed on a pile of sacks was a large tabby cat. Curled around her were the smallest kittens Roger had ever seen. Their eyes were all tightly closed. Miss Stewart and the other children were crowding into the doorway now and everyone wanted to touch the kittens but Mr Robinson shook his head.

'It's Mrs Duffy's tabby cat. It went missing a few days ago,' he told Miss Stewart, laughing. 'Wait until she knows about this.'

Mrs Duffy was one of the school cooks and she lived in the next street to the school.

'I'd better go and tell her,' said Mr Robinson, closing the woodshed door and locking it again. 'Can this lad come with me, Miss Stewart, since he's really saved Tabitha and her kittens. I wasn't going to go into the woodshed for days.'

Roger went with Mr Robinson to Mrs Duffy's house and back to the woodshed with Mrs Duffy and Mr Robinson to see Tabitha and the kittens. Mrs Duffy was carrying a tin of food, a tin opener and Tabitha's food bowl.

'We'd better leave her here for a day or two until the kittens are big enough to be moved,' said Mrs Duffy when she saw Tabitha and her babies. 'Roger, you get to school early. You can help me feed Tabitha tomorrow if you like.'

Roger did not grumble at his mother for dropping him at school too early for the next few days. He could not get there fast enough in case any of the other children arrived before he did and were given the job of feeding Tabitha and seeing the kittens.

Friendship

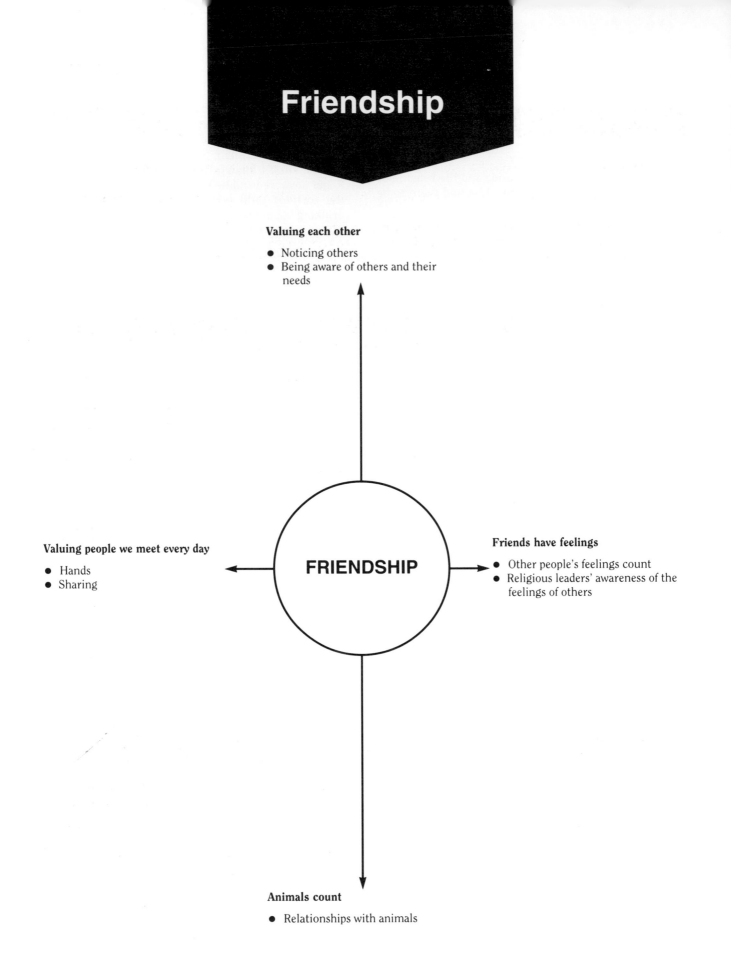

Valuing each other
- Noticing others
- Being aware of others and their needs

Valuing people we meet every day
- Hands
- Sharing

FRIENDSHIP

Friends have feelings
- Other people's feelings count
- Religious leaders' awareness of the feelings of others

Animals count
- Relationships with animals

LEARNING OBJECTIVES

- To be aware of the value of every person and to be familiar with ways in which religious communities recognise this.
- To explore relationships with one's own family and friends and to become aware of the positive and negative aspects of relationships.
- To look at examples of friendship given in sacred books: Naomi and Ruth, the Good Samaritan, Guru Nanak and Mardana, the Prophet Muhammad and his friends, Jesus and his disciples.
- To be aware of the wider contexts of friendship – to the community and in the world.

STARTING POINTS

Cix

- Give the children large sheets of drawing paper and pencils and ask them to draw a picture of a special friend, writing the name of the friend clearly on top of the picture.

- Sit informally in a circle and ask each child in turn to hold up his or her picture and say a few words about the special friend, where he or she lives, how they met and how they first became friends.

- Divide the children into pairs. Ask each child to find out as much as possible about the likes and dislikes of their partners. Let them write these under the name of their partner, on paper, and draw some of the likes and dislikes discovered. Return to the informal circle and ask each child to introduce their partner and say something about them: 'This is John. He likes football but he doesn't like running'; 'This is Michelle. She likes swimming but she doesn't like going to the shops' will be enough.

- Ask pupils if they remember who was the first person to talk to them on their first day at school. Let them write down the names of friends they made during their first few days at school and the people who are their friends now. Are they the same or not? Find out if the children can suggest why they have different friends now if this is the case.

- Let pupils practise holding hands in their circle. Ask them how this feels. Find out if each child knows the names of all the other children in the class and if they can memorise some of the likes and dislikes of others in the class. Pupils can record details of their classmates in their workbooks or on sheets of display.

- Holding hands, sing the topic song, **Friends**, and talk about the words together.

VALUING EACH OTHER

Area of study 1

C81 –84

Purpose
To emphasise the value of each child in the class and to examine ways of communicating positively with each other.

Activity 1: Noticing others
[A] Talk with the children about the importance of every child in the class. Draw and cut large paper or cardboard heads, one representing each child. Ask the children to provide words they would like to have written about themselves on the flap below their cardboard head, 'Joanne gets on well with the other children', 'Jimmy is always kind to others', and so on. Explain that everyone (including the teacher) may add good, positive comments about someone else in the class at any time. For example, they might add 'Alice lent me her crayons', 'David let me hold his tractor' at the end of the school day. A wide strip of paper on which

Joanne
Joanne gets on well with other children.
Joanne smiles a lot.

Jimmy
Jimmy is always kind to others.
Jimmy lent me his pen today.

95

to write comments could be folded into equal sections condensed under a name flap and pulled out for use. This approach avoids embarrassment for less popular pupils.

B Give out **Copymaster 81** (My promise to be ...) and read the words at the bottom of the copymaster with the children. Then discuss the word 'promise'. The children should say the words out loud and then fill in the blanks. They can then draw their own faces and hair, and colour their portraits.

C Read the story **Julie's first day at school** (p. 100) to emphasise how lonely many children might feel if they don't know anyone when they start school, then work on **Copymaster 82** (Helping a newcomer) to explore ways in which children can respond helpfully to new members of the school. With a pencil or finger, pupils should follow the sequence of pictures as they progress from the start to the finish of the school day, filling in empty squares with ideas of their own.

Now make a simple display to remind pupils of how they might help others throughout the school day.

D Divide the class into small groups and ask each group to act out a playtime experience. Draw these together afterwards and talk with the class about playtime events. Give out **Copymaster 83** (Playground survey) and ask the children, a few at a time over a period of a week, to observe what other children are doing in their school playground. Read the activities written on the copymaster first with the whole class, so they know what they are looking for before embarking upon the survey and select an additional activity to place at the foot of the sheet. They should place a tick in the boxes provided to record different activities. At the end of the week, discuss the results of the survey with the children and ask them if they had ticked the 'children on their own' boxes at all. What might they do to help these children in the playground?

E Give the children cards on which are written remarks such as 'Go away, I'm playing with Jane today', 'You can't be in our group', 'Give me a toffee', 'Don't do that or I'm telling'. Encourage children to work in groups and share their reactions to these remarks with

group members before discussing them with the whole class.

Activity 2: Being aware of others and their needs

A Record the following incidents on a tape recorder and sit with the children informally to listen to them.

● Jack and Mike were on their way home from school. They had been tossing a ball to each other and were enjoying each other's company. Suddenly a group of bigger boys appeared, took the ball and ran off with it. Jack ran after them and tried to get the ball back. One of the bigger boys pushed Jack to the floor. 'Mike!' shouted Jack. 'Mike, come and help me.'

Mike saw what was happening and he was afraid. He ran away and the big boys laughed at him.

'So much for your friend,' they said and they ran off with the ball, leaving Jack lying in the street.

● Emily was walking home after playing at her friend Anne's house. She liked Anne and her family, who always treated Emily very well. Some of Emily's and Anne's friends from school came out of a shop on the High Street.

'Hi, Emily,' they said. 'Why don't you play with us tomorrow instead of Anne? She's just a silly baby.'

'No, thanks,' answered Emily. 'And don't call Anne silly. She's my friend.'

● Ben fell over in the schoolyard and after his teacher had washed and bandaged his leg she said to him, 'I'm afraid you're going to be late for dinner, now, Ben. Shall I write a note for you so that you won't have to go to the back of the queue?'

'There's no need, thank you, Miss,' answered Ben. 'Billy will have saved me a place. He always does.'

'It's good to be able to trust a friend,' his teacher said.

Ben limped away to join the dinner queue. At the first he couldn't see Billy but then he saw a hand waving from the front of the queue.

'Come on, Ben, I saved you a place,' shouted Billy.

'Thanks, Bill.'

Ben limped to join his friend. He knew he could rely on Billy.

B Write on the board the heading 'Friendship' and ask the children for suggestions to define it: 'a friend is someone who saves a place in the dinner queue for you', 'a friend sticks up for you even when you are not there', 'a friend is someone who sometimes plays the games you want to play', etc. Talk about these and add the comment 'to have friends you have to be one'.

C Talk with the children about the less positive aspects of friendship such as quarrelling and making up afterwards or even being persuaded to do things known to be wrong by friends. Highlight these aspects of friendship by working on **Copymaster 84** (Keeping friends). Discuss the pictures with the children and ask them to tell you if they have been involved in any of the 'No!' picture situations, such as arguing, fighting and pushing. Encourage them to tell you of their experiences relating to these incidents. Now look at the pictures with them under the 'Yes!' heading. Discuss these and explain that if they react in this way in a situation they will keep their friends and be much happier. They can colour the pictures and label them using the words at the foot of the copymaster.

D Give the children pieces of paper, pencils and rulers. Help them to divide the paper into squares. Now read the following incident.

Jenny saw Rachel take an apple out of Mary's lunch box when Mary had gone to show the teacher her

work. The bell for lunchtime rang soon afterwards and Rachel took the apple into the yard with her.

'I'm telling Mary what you've done,' said Jenny.

Rachel took a bite from the apple and offered the rest of it to Jenny. 'Here. Have a bite,' she said.

The apple looked really delicious and Jenny badly wanted some of it, but she knew her friend had been wrong to take the apple.

'It's stealing,' she said.

'Oh, listen to Miss Goody-Goody,' jeered Rachel. 'Don't tell me you've never taken anything which didn't belong to you.'

Ask the children to draw this incident, step by step in the squares they have made on their papers and to draw what they think would have happened next. Remind the children of positive and negative points of being a friend and discuss whether it is necessary to agree with friends' actions and how one should respond when opinions differ.

FRIENDS HAVE FEELINGS

C85 –88

Purpose
To value other people's opinions.

Activity 1: Other people's feelings count
A Invite every child to bring a toy or possession they especially value to school and ensure that each article is well cared for. Place all the possessions on a table and sit with the children near to the display. Hold up every toy or object in turn, handling it with the utmost care and asking to whom it belongs. Stress that every child's toy is valuable and that if other children wish to handle or play with someone else's toy they must first ask the owner's permission politely and thank the owner if allowed to play with the toy.

Let the children spend some time sharing the experience of playing carefully with other children's toys. Then replace the toys on the table.

✓ Distribute **Copymaster 85** (My toy) and ask the children to use this opportunity to think about how much their own personal toy means to them and their willingness to share it with a friend.

B Read and dramatise **The blind men and the elephant** (p. 100) story and remind the children of the different ways in which each toy they brought to school was valued and treasured for different reasons.

C Read the story, **A bad start for the Watsons** (p. 101). Talk to them first about the story and ask them whether they think Jimmy Watson and his brother would greet anyone politely or pleasantly on their way to school that morning. Divide the class into groups and ask them to produce a short scene showing what might happen when the Watsons meet again that evening; whether the morning episode would be completely forgotten or whether forgiveness and saying sorry would be necessary, possibly between the two boys. Alternatively, pupils can write appropriate endings to the story, describing what happens next.

D Show the children photographs of the Hindu festival of Rakshabandham, when Hindu girls tie a coloured thread or band around their brother's wrist as a sign of love and friendship while brothers give their sisters presents as a token of love and respect. Invite Hindu children who celebrate this festival to tell the class about it and show the most recent wrist band and present they exchanged.

✓ Consider with the children how easy it is not to notice how other people are feeling and to make others feel unimportant. Look together at the six pictures on **Copymaster 86** (Do I notice?) which focus upon peoples' or animals' feelings in different situations. Then read the words at the foot of the sheet and ask children to describe the feelings depicted in each picture using the appropriate word.

E Write the name 'Zacchaeus' on the board and let the children practise saying it out loud. Tell them the story of Zacchaeus (Luke 19:1–10) explaining that he was 'out of things' because nobody liked him until Jesus came and surprised everyone by inviting himself to Zacchaeus' house for dinner. Give pupils **Copymaster 87** (Zacchaeus, the odd one out) and ask them to colour in the picture of Zacchaeus and underneath write down ways they can help other people not to feel left out of things, such as talking to someone who is on their own in the playground, or visiting a neighbour who lives on their own and is lonely. They can make a poster on the subject 'odd one out', as shown opposite.

F Read the story **The Buddha and the old monk** (p. 101) and let the children act out or draw pictures of a scene from the story.

Activity 3: Religious leaders' awareness of others' feelings

A Using sheets of card, a ruler, pencil, felt-tips and scissors, draw with the children a simple house similar to the one-storey buildings in New Testament times (see

Sacred books, p. 66). Now take a sheet of paper, fold the paper in half and then in half again. Ask pupils to draw a simple outline of four men dressed in clothes they will have seen or used in Christmas plays (see **Birth celebrations**, p. 20) and cut these out, placing all the cut-out figures in or at the door of the house. Draw and cut out figures to represent Jesus, the man on the stretcher and his four friends, as shown below.

B Sit the children around the cardboard house and tell the story of **The man with four friends** (p. 101), the children moving the figures accordingly as the story is told.

C Use **Copymaster 88** (Faith and friendship) so that the children can make their own storybook about Jacob and his four friends by looking at the pictures, colouring them in, reading the sentences and cutting them out with the pictures in the correct sequence. They then stick the pictures and matching sentences on to small pieces of sugar paper and staple the pages together in the right order to form their book, calling it 'The man with four friends'.

D Finish this Area of Study by reading **Jesus helps a friend** (p. 102) to show how sharing friendship means helping each other in times of trouble. The children can draw a picture of Rachel preparing the meal for Jesus and her family.

Daniel | Joseph | Reuben | Simon

① Draw the four friends of Jacob.

② Cut on the dotted line.

③ Fold under and stick upright, next to model of house.

98

ANIMAL FRIENDS

Purpose
To show how relationships can be formed with non-human friends.

Activity: Relationships with animals

A Invite the children to bring photographs of family pets and make a large wall chart or poster upon which all the photographs of the animals are placed and labelled with the animal's name and the child's surname, the kind of food it eats and how much it is exercised and groomed.

B Cut pictures from magazines and catalogues of family pets with the children. Divide a large sheet of paper into sections and tell pupils that each section is a cage in a pet shop. They can put the animal pictures into the right section.

C Share with the children the stories of **The lucky tortoise** and **Lola, the milk dog** (pp. 103 and 104) and let them make up their own stories about Lola and her milk round.

D Discuss the working partnership which some animals (cats, dogs, horses) have with their owners. Give the children the following short story as an example:

The Prophet Muhammad understood animals very well indeed. He owned a very special camel who was so clever that the prophet trusted the camel entirely. When he went to live in Medina the people who had invited him asked him where he would like his house to be built.

'I will let my camel choose the best spot for me,' answered Muhammad and set his camel loose in the streets of Medina and he and the leaders of the city followed the animal until it stopped in a pleasant spot just inside the city gates.

'This is where my house should be built,' said the prophet. 'My camel knew where I would like to live.'

E Read the children the story of **St Francis** (p. 104) and ask them to draw a picture of the birds sitting on his shoulders and other animals around his feet.

VALUING PEOPLE WE MEET EVERY DAY

Purpose
To appreciate the people we meet every day who perform a service for us.

Activity 1: Hands

A Make handprint paint by mixing together wallpaper paste and dry powder paint until the mixture is like thick cream. Give the children sheets of paper, scissors and a gluebrush. Ask each child to dip his or her hands into the paint and to make handprints on their sheets of paper. When the prints are dry these can be cut out and glued to larger sheets and displayed on the classroom wall.

B Use **Copymaster 89** (Helping hands) to consider ways in which we use our hands and to look at ways in which hands can reassure others and help them. Study the pictures with the children and read the words at the bottom of the copymaster. The children can then draw a line from the picture to the right descriptive word at the foot of the sheet and draw a ring around it.

C Make a list with the children of people we meet every day who do us a service by working with their hands (doctors, nurses, shop assistants, postmen and women, traffic wardens the lollipop man or lady). The children can then draw around their own hand on a sheet of paper; at the tip of the thumb and four fingers ask them to draw a sketch of these people and state how they help underneath.

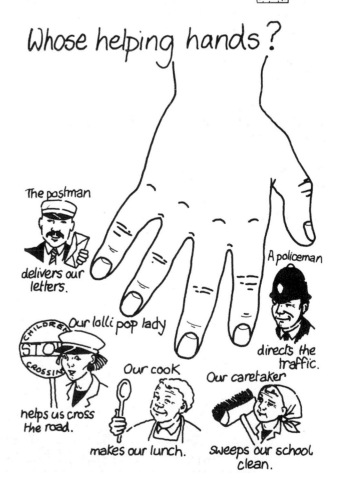

Whose helping hands?

The postman delivers our letters.

A policeman directs the traffic.

Our lolli pop lady helps us cross the road.

Our cook makes our lunch.

Our caretaker sweeps our school clean.

D Read the story **Mrs Webb, the lollipop lady** (p. 104) to introduce a discussion on how we can appreciate those who help us in our daily lives.

Activity 2: Sharing

A Divide the class into small groups and invite each group to sit around a table on which there is an apple, an orange, a bag of sweets, a toy and a jigsaw. Ask each child to choose one of the items on the table and to consider whether he or she will have the item all to themselves or whether they will share it with the group. Each item, if shared, should be carefully divided or children should have equal time to hold the toy or play with the jigsaw.

B **Copymaster 90** (Sharing) gives children the opportunity to draw various objects that they would be willing to share with their friends. They can write the name of the object, who they may share it with and comment briefly why. For example, they could write 'my teddy, Susan, she will look after it'; 'my sweets, Mummy, because she is kind', etc.

C Read the story **Guru Nanak and Brother Lalo** (p. 104) to illustrate sharing and explore ways in which poor people and countries in need can be helped.

D Read the following to the children.

Maya was 5 years old and she could not speak or hear. She had been found on the streets of the big city of Calcutta in India and she was taken to the special hospital at the Children's Orphanage which Mother Teresa, a Christian nun, had founded many years before.

In this quiet hospital where young nuns dressed in blue and white cared for her every day, Maya learned to trust people again and to hear and speak.

Revise the work done by Mother Teresa and others who are helping needy children at the present time (see **Food**, p. 30). Pupils can submit a colour sketch of the story of Maya or they can write a brief account of the ways in which they personally can help people like her.

E Sit the children in a large circle and invite them in turn to share with the class what they have learned about friendship and how they intend to be more considerate and friendly to those around them.

TOPIC STORIES ▶

Julie's first day at school

Julie was brought to school on her first day by Kate, her big sister, who was eight and in the Junior School. Kate took Julie into the cloakroom, found the peg with her name on it and hung up Julie's coat.

'See, Julie, your peg has a yellow butterfly on it,' said Kate, afraid that Julie was going to cry. 'You'll know which peg is yours from now on, won't you?'

Julie nodded and held Kate's hand tightly as they went into the big, sunny classroom where Miss Jenkins, Julie's teacher was sitting within a small group of girls and boys looking at a jigsaw.

'Hello, Julie. Welcome to Class One,' Miss Jenkins said, smiling at Julie and holding out her hand. 'Come and choose something to play with from over here.'

Kate waited until the teacher took her little sister to the play corner and then she said quickly, 'I'll see you later, Julie,' and was gone.

A girl with fair hair and a green dress was playing with some sand.

'This is Lucy,' said Miss Jenkins. 'Lucy started school today, too. Why don't you play together for a while?'

Julie and Lucy looked at each other, but said nothing. Miss Jenkins left them and went back to the other children. Julie didn't know what to say to Lucy and Lucy didn't know what to say to Julie. They both stayed by the sandpit and suddenly Lucy asked, 'Can you make a sandcastle?'

'Yes,' said Julie, and the two girls set to work.

By the time the bell went for playtime, they were friends.

The blind men and the elephant

The King of the Indian city of Varanasi had invited his wise men to a meeting. He really wanted the men to help him rule his people more wisely but instead of this they began to argue. Each wise man had a different idea about gods and sacred books and no one would listen to anyone else's opinion.

'You are all being nasty to each other,' said the King at last. 'Now, you will come with me and watch what happens.'

The wise men went with the King to the market place. The King gave an order that all the blind men in the city should be brought to him and he then asked for an elephant to be put in the midst of the blind men.

'Now,' he told the blind men, 'this is an elephant. I want each of you to go to it, feel it and tell me what this animal looks like.'

The first blind man went forward. He felt the elephant's head. The second blind man took the elephant's ear, the third its tusk, the fourth its trunk, the fifth its foot, the sixth its back, and the seventh the tuft of its tail.

'Well, what does an elephant look like?' asked the King at last.

The first blind man who had felt the elephant's head said, 'An elephant looks like a pot.'

'No, it doesn't,' argued the second blind man who had felt the elephant's ear. 'It looks like a fan.'

'Oh, that's nonsense,' cried the man who had felt the elephant's tusk. 'An elephant is round, hard and smooth, like the handle of a plough.'

'Don't be so stupid,' said the man who had felt the elephant's trunk. 'An elephant looks like a snake.'

'It's like a pillar,' shouted the man who had felt its foot.

'No, no, it's like a barn,' snapped the man who had felt the elephant's back.

'You are wrong. An elephant is like a feather duster,' the seventh man shouted who had felt the tuft of his tail.

A furious argument broke out as each blind man tried to shout the others down. Eventually they all began to fight in the market place. The city's wise men started to laugh. The King sent in some of the local men to stop the fight and then he turned to the wise men who were still laughing.

'I don't know why you are laughing, gentlemen,' he said. These poor men are ignorant and they are blind so they have some excuse for such behaviour. You are supposed to be the learned men of our city but you are worse than these men. They should have felt the whole body of the elephant before they decided what it looked like. You should examine everything from different angles, hear everyone else's ideas before you start arguing. At the moment you are considering your own narrow views only.'

With that, the King left his wise men and marched back to the palace. The wise men followed slowly. They knew their King had taught them a much-needed lesson.

A bad start for the Watsons
It was a bad day for the Watson family. The alarm clock didn't ring and everyone overslept, Mum and Dad blaming each other and the children fighting for the bathroom. Dad fell over Jimmy's football boots as he dashed for the front door and he shouted, 'Jimmy, if you don't put your things away after you've finished with them, I'll throw them in the bin.'

Jimmy was upset. Mum and Dad were always telling him to get everything he needed ready for school the night before and now he was in trouble for doing that. He was just about to go into the bathroom but when his father shouted at him, Bobby, Jimmy's elder brother got in first. Jimmy kicked the door angrily and his mother shouted, 'Jimmy, get down here and wash in the kitchen. I'm going to be late for work and you'll all miss the school bus at this rate.'

Then little Christina upset her milk all over the kitchen table and all over her clean clothes. Bobby's football shirt was dirty so he took Jimmy's and there was a fight in which Jimmy's shirt was torn.

The Buddha and the old monk
Siddartha Gautama, the old monk, once visited a monastery where he was given a lovely room all to himself. At mealtimes he met all the monks and the visitors to the monastery but the Buddha knew there was a small cell in the monastery grounds where someone lived all alone. When the Buddha asked about this person no one told him very much so one day he followed one of the monks to the cell. The monk had a bowl of rice and some water. He left these outside the cell door and went away.

The Buddha waited, hiding behind a tree. Suddenly the cell door opened and an old monk, filthy and covered in sores opened the door to take his food and water. The Buddha stepped forward and spoke to the man who was frightened because no one ever bothered to talk to him.

Some time later, the Buddha's room in the monastery was found to be empty and the monks thought he had left. When the food was taken to the old monk as usual, the Buddha opened the door. Beside him was the old monk, clean and tidy and cured from his illness.

'My friend here will move into the lovely room you got ready for me,' said the Buddha. 'And I shall stay here in this cell.'

The old monk would never be on his own and ignored again.

The man with four friends
Jacob had been ill since he was a small boy. He could not move his arms and legs and had to be carried everywhere. He had four good friends and they carried Jacob wherever he wanted to go on a small bed with ropes attached to it.

One day, Jacob heard that Jesus, the great teacher and healer was visiting Capernaum, the seaside town where Jacob lived.

'I wonder if Jesus could help me,' he thought. 'I'll ask Daniel, Joseph, Reuben and Simon if they will take me to Jesus as soon as possible.'

Usually, Jacob's friends took him to the market place or to sit outside the synagogue so that people might feel sorry for the paralysed man and give him money. They called the next afternoon and Jacob asked them, 'Have you any idea where Jesus will be today?'

'He's at his friend Peter's house,' answered Daniel,

who had seen the crowds outside Peter's house on the way to Jacob's home. 'Why do you ask?'

'I think Jesus will be able to cure me,' replied Jacob and his friends looked at each other.

'Why didn't we think of taking you to Jesus?' Joseph was excited. 'He's cured many people. We'll take you there at once.'

The four men picked up the thin ropes which were on each side of Jacob's sleeping mat and carried him through the streets of Capernaum until they reached the home of Peter, the fisherman, a close friend of Jesus.

'Oh, look,' cried Reuben in disappointment. 'We'll never get in there. They've had to leave the door open because of the crowd.'

They put Jacob on his bed on the ground as they looked at the large crowd outside Peter's house. Then Simon had a brilliant idea.

'What about the roof?' he asked. 'There will be stairs at the back of the house like there are in ours and we can push holes in the thatch and lower Jacob down.'

'Wonderful,' Daniel said and Reuben and Joseph agreed. 'What do you think, Jacob?'

'I agree – if it's not too hard for you all,' answered Jacob.

The four friends picked up Jacob's bed and carried him round to the back of Peter's house. They lifted the bed with Jacob on it and climbed carefully to the top of the stairs at the back of the house. Then Daniel climbed on to the roof. It was made of earth and thatch stretched over wooden beams. Daniel made a hole in the earth and the thatch and signalled to his friends. Carefully, they carried the sick man on to the roof.

'I've made a hole in the thatch,' explained Daniel. 'We should just be able to lower the bed through it.'

All four men lay flat on their stomachs and stared through the hole Daniel had made in the roof. Only Jesus' voice could be heard in the room below. Everyone else seemed to be listening silently but it was very clear that when Jacob was lowered into the house he would be at the front of a large crowd. Gently, Daniel and Joseph made the hole in the roof a little wider and then, helped by Simon and Reuben, they lowered Jacob and his bed down into the room below them.

Jesus had just finished speaking when he saw the eyes of everyone in the crowded room fixed on the ceiling. A few pieces of earth dropped almost at Jesus' feet and then the watching crowd gasped in astonishment. Through the roof came a bed with a man held securely on it by hands reaching through the hole in the roof. Other hands gripped ropes attached to the bed and suddenly the bed and the man lying on it arrived at Jesus' feet.

Jesus looked down at Jacob. He knew that he and the friends who had helped to get him to the front of the crowd had great faith. Smiling at Jacob he said 'Get up, take up your bed and walk.'

For a moment Jacob lay exactly where he was. Then he felt a great energy and power moving through his body. He moved his hand slowly and then more quickly. Then he sat up and managed to get to his feet. Some of the

crowd ran forward to steady Jacob as he tried to walk for the first time.

A few minutes later, Jacob was hugging Daniel, Joseph, Simon and Reuben, the friends who had taken him to Jesus.

Jesus helps a friend

It was the Sabbath Day in Capernaum and Jesus, the teacher and healer from Nazareth, was going to the synagogue with all his friends. Peter and Andrew, the two fishermen brothers who had become Jesus' close friends, were overjoyed that Jesus should be visiting their synagogue because they knew as a visiting teacher (rabbi), he would be asked to read from the holy scriptures.

'He and the others can come back to our house afterwards and have a meal,' Peter said to Andrew. 'Rachel will be only too pleased to help Sarah prepare for Jesus' visit. You know how Rachel loves Jesus.'

Andrew nodded and smiled. Rachel was Peter's mother-in-law and she always made Peter's friends welcome. She loved to have Jesus to visit the family and would spend hours preparing special dishes for him.

It was a wonderful service in the synagogue. Jesus had read so clearly and firmly from the Scriptures that people were saying, 'This man really means every word he reads'. Peter felt proud because Jesus and several of their friends were going back to his house for a meal.

When they reached the house which Peter, his wife and their family shared with Rachel, his mother-in-law and Andrew, Peter's brother, no one came out to greet them and the house was not full of cooking smells as it usually was. No one seemed to have cooked anything at all.

'Something has happened,' Peter said anxiously. 'I'm sorry your meal doesn't seem to be ready. Please sit down and I'll find out what is going on.'

'Don't worry, Peter,' said Jesus quietly. 'I'm sure all will be well.'

Sarah, Peter's wife came into the room. She was pale and had been crying.

'What is it, Sarah?' asked Peter. 'Is one of the children ill?'

'No. It's mother,' answered Sarah, tearfully. 'It was just after you left to go to the synagogue. She was cooking the meal – said she wanted to do it herself today. She suddenly fainted and she's just lying on her bed now, unable to do anything.'

'Have you sent for the doctor?' asked Peter.

'How can I? It's the Sabbath. Doctor's won't come out on the Sabbath.'

Peter turned to Jesus. 'Lord, is there anything you can do, please? Rachel is very dear to all of us and she loves you very much.'

'Yes, of course I will help if I can.' Jesus was smiling at Peter and as Sarah turned to lead Jesus to her mother's small room, Jesus pressed her shoulder gently.

'I'm sure your mother will soon be well again,' he said and he followed Sarah into Rachel's room.

As soon as Rachel saw Jesus she held out her hand to him and he took it, smiling down at her lovingly.

'You are better now, Rachel,' Jesus said gently. 'You have been working too hard. You won't be ill like this ever again.'

Rachel sat up and hugged Jesus. 'I'm feeling better already,' she told him. 'You must be really hungry. I'll have to get on with your meal right away.'

Jesus laughed and said there was no hurry but Rachel was up and hurrying to the main room where everyone gave shouts of delight and wanted her to sit down and rest.

'Certainly not,' said Rachel, firmly. 'I feel better now than I have felt for years and it is Jesus, our friend, who has made me well. Now I must see to this meal for you all.'

'Let her do as she wishes,' advised Jesus to Peter and Sarah started to rush after Rachel.

Some time later Jesus and his friends were enjoying the best meal they had had for a long time with Rachel, happy and cheerful as usual, helping Sarah to wait on them at the table, something she loved to do as the mother of the house.

The lucky tortoise

Mr and Mrs Yates and their three children, Marianne, Jonathan and Elizabeth, were going on holiday. The children were looking forward to going away but they were worried about Edward, their pet tortoise.

'Supposing he crawls away and gets out of the garden,' little Elizabeth said anxiously.

'We'll ask Mrs Barnes to look after him,' her mother told her. 'She has Fred, her own tortoise, and the two of them can play together.'

Mrs Barnes agreed and the children took Edward to her the day they went away. They liked to visit Mrs Barnes because she had a small fishpond in her garden. The children liked to sit quietly and gaze at the fish, as they swam around the pond. Fred did not seem to like Edward, though. He ran at him and butted Edward with his head.

'That's enough, Fred,' said Mrs Barnes, sternly. 'Edward is your guest and you must make him welcome.'

'Will they be alright?' asked Jonathan, anxiously. 'Will they fight?'

'Oh, no, they'll soon get used to each other,' answered Mrs Barnes. 'You see, Fred has been the only tortoise here for years and he's jealous of Edward.'

'Edward is old, as old as Mummy,' said Marianne. 'We don't like to leave him but we can't take him in the car.'

'He'll be fine. You go off now and enjoy yourselves,' smiled Mrs Barnes, walking with the children to the front door.

Fred, Mrs Barnes' tortoise, glared at Edward. 'You wait. I'm going to knock you into that fishpond,' he threatened.

Poor Edward had a dreadful time in the next few days. Whenever Mrs Barnes caught Fred thumping Edward with his shell she shouted at him and put Edward in another part of the garden, but as soon as her back was turned, Fred would start again.

'Not long to go now, Edward,' said Mrs Barnes one morning, as she put fresh lettuce leaves on the grass for the tortoises. 'Your family will be back tonight.'

There was no sign of Fred and Edward was munching his lettuce happily when suddenly Fred banged him from behind with his shell. Edward nearly choked and moved out of the way but Fred followed him.

'I'm leaving tonight,' said Edward. 'The children will come to get me as soon as they arrive home.'

'Well, they won't find you,' sneered Fred and he banged Edward again. Edward banged Fred back and the two tortoises were fighting so loudly that Edward did not realise they were getting nearer to the fishpond. By the time Edward did realise it, Fred had given him a hard push with his head and poor Edward fell into the pond. Down he went to the bottom of the pond and Fred looked over the edge of the pond but could not see him.

'Fred! Look what you've done!' cried Mrs Barnes, running out of the house. Fred crept away into the bushes and Mrs Barnes looked in vain for Edward, but she couldn't see him.

There was a ring at her doorbell and when the frantic Mrs Barnes answered the door, she found Mr Yates, the children's father, on her doorstep.

'We came back early, because the children were so worried about Edward,' he explained. 'I'll take him now, if you don't mind.'

Mrs Barnes burst into tears as she tried to tell Mr Yates what had happened. He went with her to the pond and in the end, he took off his shoes and socks, rolled up his trousers and climbed into the pond. He moved very slowly until his foot kicked against something hard. He bent down at once and lifted a dripping tortoise out of the water.

'He's dead,' he said, sadly. 'Whatever will my wife and the children say?'

Just then the children arrived. As soon as they saw Edward they began to cry and Mr Yates shook Edward impatiently.

'Why did you have to die just when we'd come back to get you?' he asked angrily.

Edward sneezed and as the children crowded round he began to shake his head and move his legs.

'He's alive!' cried Mr Yates. 'Look, you three – Edward is going to be alright!'

Of course, Edward had to be taken to the vet who said that as soon as Edward had fallen into the water he had hibernated – gone to sleep inside his shell. He would need a lot of warmth and loving care but he would recover fully from his adventure in the end.

No one was very pleased with Fred who was so frightened that he stayed in the bushes in Mrs Barnes' garden for days.

'Why did you do it, Fred?' asked Mrs Barnes, over and over again.

Fred couldn't tell her that he had done it because he was so jealous of Edward that he didn't want another tortoise in his garden.

Lola, the milk dog

Lola was a lively young Alsatian who belonged to an elderly man named Jack. Jack took Lola to the park every morning and evening and she had a wonderful time running on the grass and playing with other dogs.

One day, Jack became ill and Lola had to go into kennels nearby until her master was well again. Jack was worried about her and told Brian, the milkman, who had always been friends with Lola.

'I think I'm going to have to look for another home for Lola,' he said sadly. 'I can't take her out like I used to to do and she needs a good run every day.'

Brian felt sorry for both Jack and Lola and he thought about the great love and friendship there was between the old man and his dog.

'I've got an idea, Jack,' he told the old man one morning. 'I'll take Lola with me on my milk round every morning if you like. She can sit in the van when I deliver the milk and I'll stop by the park on my way back and give her a run.'

Jack was delighted and so was Lola. She made friends with everyone on her way round the houses and shops and no one ever tried to take any milk from the back of the van when Brian was delivering – something which had happened before Lola helped with the milk round.

St Francis

Francis was the son of a rich family and he had all the money, clothes and possessions he ever wanted.

When he was still quite young, he began to give all his good clothes away to the poor boys of the town in Italy where he lived. Naturally his parents were angry and they told Francis to stop doing this.

Francis took no notice and in the end he had to leave his rich home and live in the streets and woods. He told everyone that God loved them and that they must do as Jesus told them to do – share everything they had with the poor people.

At first only the animals and birds listened to Francis. They followed him everywhere, the birds sitting on his shoulders and singing for him. Francis called them his 'little brothers and sisters'.

Other men joined Francis and they wore brown robes with ropes around their waists. They were known as Franciscans.

Francis later became St Francis, the patron saint of all animals.

Mrs Webb, the lollipop lady

Mrs Webb stood by the crossing at Willowfield School for 5 years. She always had a smile for everyone and the children loved her. Very few of them ever remembered to say 'thank you' though, and because of this, Mrs Webb didn't really know if she was important to the children or not.

One day, Mrs Webb had a fall in the street and she had to be taken to hospital. She was unable to go to work for several weeks and it was then that the children really missed her. Another lollipop lady came to Willowfield but the children missed Mrs Webb, even though they liked Mrs Jones, the new lady.

'What can we do to show Mrs Webb that we love her and miss her?' the Headteacher of Willowfield School asked the children in assembly one morning. The children went back to their classrooms and each class found a different way of thanking Mrs Webb and telling her they missed her.

When Mrs Webb was visited by some of the children, all carrying cards, flowers and drawings for her she knew that everyone really had loved her. She got better very quickly after that and was soon back in her old place at the crossing by Willowfield School.

Guru Nanak and Brother Lalo

Guru Nanak began the Sikh religion but he had been a Hindu of high caste and whenever he went into towns and villages, the rich men of the area would try to get Nanak to stay with them. Guru Nanak always stayed with the first person who invited him whether that person was rich or poor.

In one village a poor carpenter called Lalo was the first to invite Guru Nanak to stay.

'Thank you. I'd love to stay with you,' answered Guru Nanak, smiling at Lalo.

Later, when Nanak had finished speaking with the visitors, some rich Muslims arrived.

'Malik Bhago wants you to stay with him tonight,' they told the Guru.

'Please thank him but I'm already staying with Lalo,' replied Guru Nanak.

'Staying with that poor carpenter? He lives in a mean hut and he eats black bread only,' cried the rich men. 'Malik Bhago is the city Governor and he has invited you to his comfortable home.'

'Thank him, please, but I am staying with Lalo,' answered Guru Nanak, walking away towards Lalo's hut.

Guru Nanak often got into trouble with the well-known people of the towns and villages he visited because he would not refuse an invitation given in friendship, however poor a home may be.

BIBLIOGRAPHY

Bachelor, Mary, *The Lion Christmas Book*, Lion

Bastide, Derek, *Good Practice in Primary RE*, Falmer Press

Carr, Frank, *School Assembly Stories*, Foulsham

Development Education Centre (Gillett Centre, Bristol Road, Selly Oak, Birmingham), *Start with a Story*

Goring, Rosemary, *A Dictionary of Beliefs and Religions*, Chambers Press

Gower, Ralph, *Religious Education at the Primary Stage*, Lion

Helldorfer, M. C., *Daniel's Gift*, Simon & Schuster

Hull, John (et al.) *A Gift for a Child*

Jarvis, Judy, *He was the King of the World Ever Since*, Chester House Publishing Co.

Lawton, Clive, *I am a Jew*, Franklin Watts

Palmer and Breuilly, *Religious Education and Life*, Collins

Parmiter, Ruth and Price, Monica, *A World of Light* (multi-faith book and music cassette for Primary assemblies), Schofield & Sims

Parmiter, Ruth and Price, Monica, *Guru Nanak and the Snake* (multi-faith book and music cassette for Primary assemblies), Cassell

Paulo, Tomie de, *The Clown of God*, Methuen

Peirce, Elizabeth, *Activity Assemblies for Multi-racial Schools*, Falmer Press

SHAP, *World Religions in Education*, SHAP

Watson, Brenda, *Priorities in Religious Education*, Falmer Press

FAITHS INDEX

Throughout **Blueprints** *Religious Education Key Stage 1* you will see a considerable number of activities, stories and copymasters relating to the different major faiths of the world. In order to help you locate and use specific material on each of the faiths, the following index of material has been provided.

You will also find a substantial bank of ideas and copymasters on Christmas in **Blueprints** *Christmas Key Stage 1* and **Blueprints** *Christmas Key Stage 2*; on Easter, Harvest and Thanksgiving in **Blueprints** *Festivals*.

Copymaster 37: Hindu temple I-spy
Story, pp. 47–8: Seeva's story
Copymaster 43: Prayer objects
Activity 2E, p. 56: Hindus at prayer
Activity 2E, p. 59: Hindu dress
Copymasters 48 and 49: Community clothes 1 and 2
Copymaster 50: World believers
Activity 1A–D, p. 67: Sacred books of India
Story, pp. 71–2: Rama and Sita
Activity 2A–C, p. 67: Introducing the *Mahabharata* and
  Bhavagad Gita
Story, p. 79: The Hindu creation story
Activity 2A, pp. 77–8: Diwali
Copymaster 70: Faith and new beginnings
Activity 1B, p. 86: Holi
Activity 1D, p. 98: Rakshabandham

You will also find a substantial bank of ideas and copymasters on the Hindu festival of Diwali in **Blueprints** *Festivals*.

Islam

Story, pp. 12–13: The Prophet Muhammad and the lady with the rubbish
Activity 1B, p. 9: Praying
Activity 2, p. 21: Muhammad and Mecca
Story, p. 24: The Prophet Muhammad's birth
Activity 2D, p. 34: Eid-ul-Fitr
Activity 1A–B, p. 41: Looking at a mosque
Copymaster 34: Building a mosque
Story, p. 47: The Prophet Muhammad
Copymaster 43: Prayer objects
Activity 2B–C, pp. 55–6: Muslims at prayer
Activity 2F, pp. 59–60: Muslim dress
Copymasters 48 and 49: Community clothes 1 and 2
Copymaster 50: World believers
Activity 1, pp. 67–8: Looking at the Qur'an
Copymaster 59: Muhammad
Story, p. 72: Reading from the Qur'an
Activity 1D, p. 99: Muhammad and animals

You will also find a substantial bank of ideas and copymasters on Ramadan in **Blueprints** *Festivals*.

Judaism

Activity 2C, p. 6: Jewish festivals
Activity 1B, p. 9: Praying
Story, pp. 24–5: The birth of Moses
Copymasters 19 and 20: Four special births 1 and 2
Activity 2A–C, p. 34: Food for Jewish celebrations
Activity 4, pp. 44–6: The Jewish synagogue and the importance of prayer

Story, pp. 48–9: The last plague
Story, p. 49: The escape
Copymaster 38: The Ten Commandments
Copymaster 39: Plan of a synagogue
Copymaster 40: Listen and answer
Copymaster 43: Prayer objects
Story, pp. 49–50: Jacob in the synagogue
Story, p. 50: Jacob meets Rachel and Leah
Story, pp. 50–1: Naomi goes to the synagogue
Activity 2C, p. 54: The Ten Commandments
Activity 2G–H, p. 56: Jews at prayer
Copymasters 48 and 49: Community clothes 1 and 2
Story, pp. 60–1: The Ten Commandments
Copymaster 50: World believers
Story, p. 61: Jesus' Bar Mitzvah
Activity 1A–D, p. 68: Revising the Ten Commandments and introducing the Talmud
Activity 2A–G, pp. 68–9: Looking at the Torah
Story, p. 72: The tattooed Torah
Copymaster 60: Synagogue I-spy
Copymaster 61: The seven days of creation
Activity, 1B–C, p. 74: The creation story from Genesis
Story, p. 79: The creation story from Genesis
Story, p. 80: Noah and the rainbow

You will also find a substantial bank of ideas and copymasters on the Jewish new year in **Blueprints** *Festivals*.

Sikhism

Copymaster 14: Church or temple?
Activity 2E, p. 18: Sikh naming ceremony
Activity 5A–D, pp. 21–2: Baby Nanak
Story, p. 25: The birth of Guru Nanak
Copymasters 19 and 20: Four special births 1 and 2
Story, p. 23: Ranjit is named
Activity 2E, p. 34: Sikh celebrations
Copymaster 27: Helping hand
Story, pp. 35–6: The bargain
Activity 2A–D, p. 42: Looking at a gurdwara
Copymaster 35: Gurdwara I-spy
Copymaster 43: Prayer objects
Activity 2F, p. 56: Sikhs at prayer
Activity 2D, p. 59: Sikh dress
Copymasters 48 and 49: Community clothes 1 and 2
Copymaster 50: World believers
Activity 1, p. 69–70: Looking at the Guru Granth Sahib
Story, p. 72: The temple at Amritsar
Activity 2A, p. 78: Baisakhi
Copymaster 70: Faith and new beginnings
Activity 1, p. 78: How to make a fresh start
Story, pp. 81–2: Sajjan the robber
Story, p. 104: Guru Nanak and Brother Lalo